The

How Byju's Took Indian Edtech
for a Ride

Pradip K. Saha

JUGGERNAUT BOOKS
C-I-128, First Floor, Sangam Vihar, Near Holi Chowk,
New Delhi 110080, India

First published by Juggernaut Books 2023

10 9 8 7 6 5 4 3 2 1

P-ISBN: 9789353452322
E-ISBN: 9789353453138

Typeset in Adobe Caslon Pro by R. Ajith Kumar, Noida

Printed at Thomson Press India Ltd

To Abhigyaan Rao Saha

You can move mountains, believe me, let's go.
And I will be in your corner, every day and then tomorrow.

Contents

Author's Note

This book emerged out of sheer curiosity.

Back in December 2019, during our winter break from publication, my editor at The Morning Context, Ashish K. Mishra, and I were talking about the sectors we needed to track in the coming year. We had launched The Morning Context three months before and were shaping our coverage of sectors, blissfully unaware of how our lives were going to change in four months.

One of the sectors Ashish was very keen on covering was education technology. It was the sunshine sector, he said. Investors across the world were waking up to the potential of Indian edtech and making a beeline for the start-ups in the space. There were good reasons for that.

Education in India is not just about gaining knowledge or worldly wisdom or learning skills. Eight decades after independence, education, at the most basic level, remains a dream for hundreds of millions of Indians. A dream, a tool, a bridge to a better shot at life. For the hundreds of millions of have-nots in India, education is an individualistic urge for the collective betterment of the family. So parents will sacrifice a lot in the hopes of giving their children a shot at a better life.

Our education system is broken. Schools don't have the infrastructure, the curriculum is dated, most teachers are unqualified, untrained and ill-fitted for the job, and so on. Put all this together and education becomes an evergreen, multibillion-dollar opportunity in India. The problem is, you can make millions of dollars by selling snake oil in the name of education.

These factors have fuelled the private coaching industry in India for decades. Edtech's promise was to disrupt this system and democratize education. The opportunity was huge. The money was flowing. At The Morning Context, we started out by taking stock of things. Reams were written about companies raising funds at exorbitant valuations. But where was the money going? What was the learning outcome? No one was asking these questions.

A friend once shared an experience with me. They worked in the communications team at an education company and had reached out to a business journalist to explore a story. The potential story was about visiting the schools they were working with to sit in classrooms, and experience the impact of their programmes. The journalist, my friend told me, asked how much money the company had raised. It wasn't about the money, it was about an initiative and its impact, my friend said. 'Sorry, no funding, no story,' the journalist had responded.

But we wanted to go beyond the funding game and look deeper. And, we started with Byju's because it was, and still is, the largest company in the sector in terms of valuation. It raised more money than all the other edtech players combined; it employed the largest number; and it had the most subscriptions. Therefore, it was also the bellwether and the trendsetter for the sector. Whatever it did, others followed. Investors saw it as the safest bet and herd instinct kicked in. If A has invested, B will come, and then C will feel the FOMO and rush in. It meant that Byju's didn't even need to worry about investors doing full due diligence before signing off with an investment.

In short, edtech was, and still is to a large extent, all about Byju's. The friend quoted above recalls the ironic jokes about being 'Byju-ed away' at investor meetings. 'That's all fine but how are you different from Byju's?' investors would ask. At one meeting, they were Byju-ed away within minutes.

But what about the students? We started talking with parents who had subscribed to these companies, teachers and industry experts to understand the efficacy of the products in the market. What we learnt was appalling. There was no way to measure the efficacy of the products or learning outcomes. I spoke with hundreds of parents, most of whom thought they were trapped. Children had already lost interest in the product and the tablet Byju's handed out as a part of the package was being used to play games. Byju's, these parents told me, was all about sales masquerading as education.

Then Covid-19 struck, and online became the only mode for learning and edtech took off. But the hypergrowth created a bubble and now companies that had received a flood of investment and expanded operations with a focus on pure growth are crumbling under the weight of losses and looking at drastically reduced demand.

We kept at our investigations, peeling layer after layer to get to the bottom of the edtech mess. It was September 2022, and we were chatting about something else, when Chiki Sarkar at Juggernaut asked me if I had someone in mind who could do a book about Byju's. We had just broken the stories about phantom funding in Byju's and the toxic work culture at the company. It had recently published lacklustre numbers for FY21 and the company was headed for more trouble.

'Just an honest, well-reported book on the business . . . And I guess telling a bigger story about the start-up culture here, pressures to grow at any rate, etc.,' she said.

Now, I have never asked her this, but when I see this conversation in hindsight, it probably was her way to put the seeds of the idea in my mind.

I was thrilled, I won't lie, but I was also petrified. Though we had written a lot about the company, a book sounded like a daunting task. Besides, there was work and a young child who needed his parents' attention. Did I have the bandwidth to take this up?

But if not now, when? If not this, what?

I first went to Ashish for advice. We were the best placed to do the book, he told me. 'Tu dekh, karna hai to kar le (You think about it, do it if you want to). We will manage the rest,' he said. I got the same answer from my wife, Namrata; sometimes I wonder how my editor and my wife always have similar ideas. I was still not sure. I reached out to friends who had written books and worked in the publishing industry. They all said the same thing.

A brief conversation with Prem Panicker sealed the deal.

'Doesn't matter if the story has been said before. Say it again, the whole story, in a way that is consumable for everyone,' he said. 'You know the beginning and the middle. The end will come on the way. Go for it.'

So I did. And here it is.

Over the last four years, I have spoken with hundreds of

people connected to the industry – salespersons, management, investors and above all customers – and recorded their insights and impressions. Some of them were willing to go on record. Others are still working in the industry or they have hostages to fortune, in the sense that they have children who are signed up for edtech courses. In these cases, I've used pseudonyms because the reader-recall is better if you say 'Amit' rather than 'a salesperson who requested anonymity'.

There are merits to online learning and it probably is the future of education. But what would be the model? The pedagogy, content and delivery? How do we ensure its efficacy? All these questions need to be answered first. No one in India has been able to make a sound, profitable business centred around online learning. Not yet at least. Certainly not Byju's. In fact, the misadventures of the company, one entrepreneur told me, have eroded the trust of people in online education.

In our effort to answer the questions we asked four years ago – where was the money going and where were the learning outcomes – I stumbled upon the dark underbelly of edtech, learning on the way how the biggest edtech company could become the biggest write-down in India's tech start-up history.

In another context, an Indian politician once said, 'When a big tree falls, the ground shakes'. The crash in Byju's has caused a seismic upheaval across the edtech industry. This is the story of how Byju Raveendran built his empire and how it turned into a trainwreck.

Prologue

'Our core business is the most profitable one, more than any other company in our portfolio.'

This was 10 November 2022 and we were in the middle of a two-hour-long marathon meeting in a second-floor conference room at Byju's office in IBC Knowledge Park, Bengaluru, when Byju Raveendran dropped this surprising factoid on me. For a moment, I thought I had misheard him. I could only muster a 'hmm' in response.

Raveendran said this with so much confidence that it was difficult not to believe him. Moreover, he backed up this bald statement with a glib explanation. 'It just doesn't look that way because all the costs are sitting there. The costs of all six businesses are sitting in the core business. We are creating content and products from the core business. We are not spending on our learning app. The team you will meet outside – they are creating content for something else.'

But over the past few years, Ashish, my editor at The Morning Context, and I had read Byju's earnings reports several times to know, or at least to strongly suspect, that this wasn't the case. Or at least, the auditors didn't seem to think so.

The company hadn't turned a profit in years. In fact, for FY21, the company booked a record net loss of ₹4,588 crore, almost 19 times the loss made in the previous fiscal. Yet, I thought it was futile to argue with the man, for two main reasons:

First, the numbers I had were outdated. We were in November 2022, discussing business figures for a 12-month period that ended in March 2021. The man is a maths teacher and an entrepreneur, who scaled a part-time tutorial into a $22 billion behemoth in little over a decade. Surely, he knew the numbers better and he certainly knew the current situation in the company better.

Second – and this is my opinion based on the many number of times we have spoken over the phone in the last couple of years – you can't win an argument with Raveendran. He will have an answer and an explanation for everything. So, I decided to drop it and move on with the conversation, leaving it to time and the auditors to arbitrate the question.

Before meeting Raveendran, I had met with another edtech executive, who has known Raveendran well for years. We were talking about edtech in general and he told me how the markets were depressed because there was no money coming in. In fact, he told me there could be a sectoral collapse in about eighteen months. As was the nature of such freewheeling chats those days, the conversation moved on to Byju's and its disastrous FY21 results.

'The best-case scenario for him will be to take Aakash public and focus on that. There isn't much left in Byju's anyway,' this person had said.

So, as soon as I left the building and booked the cab for

the airport, I called the edtech executive to tell him what I had learnt.

'I don't know why he keeps saying these things. He knows people are not going to believe him anyway. It would be better to come out clean, admit the mistakes in the business, take the valuation hit and rebuild,' the edtech executive told me. 'I was talking to him a few days ago and he kept telling me the same things he told you. At this point, it is difficult to say if he is not able to see things for what they are or putting up a brave face. Is he being defiant? Or just delusional?'

This conversation has stayed with me.

By the time January 2023 came around, it was clear that the company was suffering from a severe working capital crisis. Vendor payments and TDS returns had been delayed for months. The company had taken out a huge unsecured loan from Aakash Educational Services Limited (AESL). Also, instead of cancelling subscriptions for customers who wanted to cancel and refunding the money to Non-Banking Financial Companies, or NBFCs, which had financed the subscriptions, the company had continued to pay EMIs on behalf of the customer. There was no cash in the system.

Still, Raveendran was defiant. In an interview on the sidelines of The World Economic Forum 2023 in Davos, he told the reporter that the worst was over for the company and it was moving 'towards a sustainable long-term year of growth with strong fundamentals, so 2023 is going to be a much, much better year for us in terms of both India as well as some core segments'. FY22 and FY23 numbers are not out yet, but things are very different on the ground.

In the months following that interview, the Byju's story

has unravelled fast. The company hasn't been able to raise fresh equity capital and is embroiled in legal battles across three cities in the US with lenders of a term loan. Back home, the core online business is not generating any cash and the offline tuition centres are becoming another albatross around the company's neck. WhiteHat Jr continues to be a black hole and Byju's is milking Aakash dry. Things became so ugly that Aakash CEO Abhishek Maheshwari had to resign.

When we wrote that story for The Morning Context, the company chose its words well in its reply to our questions. 'The CEO and CFO continue to serve AESL in their current roles,' it said. This was 30 July 2023. Maheshwari left the company by the August end.

Amused at the turn of events, I went back to the source who had given me the tip about Maheshwari's departure. It was amazing how a company can make misstatements in official responses like this, I told him. This wasn't the first time either.

'I am surprised that you are still surprised,' the source texted back. 'You are a journalist, lying to you is okay. But lying to all employees, most senior leadership, even people who have access to accounts . . . you even tell them we are profitable – that is another level.'

This was one of the rare occasions I didn't have a good comeback.

Defiance is an essential quality in a leader. Deception – exaggeration, careful omission, half-truths and lies – may also be a part of running a business. American economist and social scientist Thorstein Veblen considered lying an essential part of American capitalism. '[T]he arts of business are the arts of bargaining, effrontery, salesmanship, [and] make believe and are directed to the gain of the business man at the cost of the community, at large and in detail,' he wrote in his final book *Absentee Ownership and Business Enterprise in Recent Times* (1923).

Whenever I think of Byju's the company, my mind goes back to the November 2022 conversation and a dozen similar telephonic conversations I had had before and after that meeting. The fundamental question with Byju's, after 15 years of its existence, is whether the company has moved the needle in terms of education in India. When I asked Raveendran this question, he replied in his usual fashion with, 'Much better than anyone else globally.'

Notice the careful wording. In comparing his business with others without any objective detail, Raveendran gives an answer while actually telling you nothing.

'Have we changed the landscape of education? . . . Governments have spent billions of dollars over decades, but it is very inefficient because they invest in infrastructure. They don't spend on content. Even if you create infrastructure, you can't do much. We have done better than others. Still, there is a long way to go,' he added.

A little later in the conversation, I asked him why there were so many complaints against the company from parents.

'You have a selection bias,' he told me. 'Even if 5% of dissatisfied parents take to social media, it will look like a big problem, but it is only 5%. And you will talk to only those parents that are complaining. Happy parents won't talk to you. There is a huge difference between perception and reality. Because if you are right, then I have to believe that all our investors are idiots. I will give you a dump of data for our paid customers. You randomly choose the numbers and call them and take feedback.'

No, Raveendran didn't provide me with a 'data dump' of contact details – this would arguably have been a major privacy violation anyway.

'There are complaints that sales are aggressive, but parents actually like that. High-quality graduates spending two hours with them, explaining our product, so they don't do an impulse purchase . . .' he said.

This assertion runs quite contrary to what I have learnt from my four years of reporting on the company. I might have only spoken with a few hundred salespeople and parents, but I feel confident that it's a fairly representative sample without much in the way of selection bias. Every one of them told me that if a home visit lasted that long, it only meant that the salesperson was trying to hard-sell. The company changed the sales model from home visits to teleconferencing in December 2022.

Then I asked Raveendran about WhiteHat Jr.

'There is tremendous feedback from paid users. Only armchair critics have negative comments about WhiteHat Jr,' he told me. 'The product didn't fail; the go-to-market strategy didn't work.'

I asked him about Sumeru Ventures and its phantom funding. Raveendran maintained that his company had been the victim. But how did a company the size of Byju's not do due diligence on an investor?

'We heard they invested in several unicorns,' he told me.

'But the money didn't land in any of them,' I said.

'How would we know that?'

Bankers, other investors, entrepreneurs, word-of-mouth, even just a search on the internet?

'There was no banker involved. I asked our investors and they said Sumeru was a good investor and had given term sheets to other unicorns as well.'

What happened to the plan to go public via a merger with a special-purpose acquisition company (SPAC)?

'The markets turned. No one has been able to raise. Hardly any company has gone public.'

Then there was the question of layoffs. Raveendran insisted his company had only let go of 2,500 people in October and reiterated that I had got the story wrong, which had suggested that the company had fired more than 12,000 people.

'I trust my sources,' I said.

'But how? I can assure you we didn't fire more than 2,500 people. Do you have data from EPFO [Employees Provident Fund Organisation]? I signed the paycheques. I can show you data for September, October and November.'

The data never came. I didn't have EPFO evidence at the time, but after a few months, I sourced the data that showed the company had fired far more people during that round of job cuts than they had claimed. So I asked him over one of our calls and this time I told him that I had sourced the data from EPFO.

'That is a mistake. You see, the numbers are down because we moved a lot of people from payroll to contracts,' Raveendran said.

As I said before, it is hard to argue with the man, even

if you have the evidence. There are several layers to Byju Raveendran, the businessman. He sounds vulnerable in interviews with YouTube influencers, but when asked the hard questions, he is confident and defiantly refutes any allegations against the company. His words seem heartfelt, and his pain sincere, in emails to employees about job cuts. No more cuts, he would promise. And then, Byju's would fire another tranche of thousands of employees.

———

When you meet, the first thing you notice about Raveendran is his bulked-up appearance. He's toned and fit, and clearly works out regularly, making him look a lot younger than his 40-odd years.

Once you look past his muscles, the next thing you notice is that he is always in a hurry. He talks fast, thinks faster, his eyes move constantly, taking note of every movement, looking for any change of expression in the person sitting opposite. He's always thinking ahead and considering taking the conversation in multiple possible directions – like a problem in multivariate calculus or a physics equation – and figuring out responses for all possible scenarios. When he's under pressure, this makes him look fidgety and impatient.

This impatience arises from an apparent ability to process information quicker than most people. This ability to look ahead has helped him build an empire. At the peak of the pandemic, when the company was in hyperactive mode, the joke in the industry was that someday Byju's would buy the Central Board of Secondary Education.

An incident that played out at an afterparty during the ASU+GSV Summit – the largest annual edtech event in the world – in San Diego in April 2022 illustrates the industry's attitude to Byju's in its heyday.

Byju's was everywhere at that event and, naturally, so were the people associated with it. One man from their US operations shook hands with another person, asking if they too were from another arm of Byju's. To this, a third person, a top executive in one of Byju's subsidiaries, smiled and said: 'No, not yet.' All three cracked up with laughter, as an eyewitness told me later.

As things turned out, this unbridled growth now looks like a pack of cards, stacked precariously over the last 15 years to build a house that's ready to come tumbling down.

The art of lying may be a useful skill in business or in diplomacy or politics. A lie can consist of misdirection or misstatement or overpromising. They are like verbal steroids, effective in the short term but with potentially terrible side effects in the long run. Josef Goebbels famously said that if you repeat a lie often enough, it becomes the truth. The danger is that the speaker also starts believing in the lie and history is proof that companies as well as political regimes built on a foundation of lies eventually fail terribly and loudly.

Raveendran came from nothing. He built an empire by selling a big dream to millions of people. As I discovered over the four years I covered it, the industry was all about Byju's. It was not only the biggest player with over 58,000 employees at its peak. It also had the biggest war chest and it was constantly on the lookout for acquisitions.

Any strategy that Byju's implemented, any tweak to its business model, meant a pivot for the entire industry. It was that big and that dominant. And now that the empire is coming apart at the seams because a large part of the foundation consisted of flim-flam, it might take the entire industry down with it.

1

A Dream Is Born

The year is 2013, and the place is New Delhi. The Indira Gandhi Indoor Stadium is packed to the brim to well beyond its rated capacity of 14,000-odd – there are people packed into the galleries, standing in the aisles and overflowing on to the arena. Right at the centre, there is an elevated platform surrounded by huge screens. All spotlights, and there are dozens of them, are focused at the centre of the platform. This could be a rock concert.

Out comes the artist, amidst thunderous applause. He takes a moment to soak in the atmosphere and acknowledge the crowd. He knows his audience. He knows his craft. He is confident. For the next hour or so, he is the only one who speaks, his intonations following the movements of his hands as he holds the unwavering attention of the audience with remarkable ease.

This is not a religious guru expounding on philosophy. Nor is it a musician. He is a teacher, teaching mathematics.

Later on, interviewers have often asked Byju Raveendran whether he was nervous the first time he taught a stadium full of students. He wasn't, he says. He was excited. 'To hold the attention of 25,000 students at one go,' Raveendran is often quoted as saying, 'one has to do a maths concert.'

It is an art. Once you are on the stage and all the cameras, spotlights, and 50,000 eyes are focused on you, it is all about the performance. Raveendran perfected this – the art of teaching at scale and holding large, live audiences captive. He built India's largest education technology business on the back of this skill.

Byju Raveendran (we will refer to him from now on just as Raveendran, even though that is really his father's name in order to avoid confusion with the eponymous company) was born in 1980 to two teachers who lived in the coastal village of Azhikode, around 7 km north of Kannur in North Kerala – an idyllic place where the Valapattanam River meets the Arabian Sea.

He studied in the local government school where his parents, Raveendran and Shobhanavalli, taught physics and maths, respectively, and where the language of instruction was Malayalam. After finishing eighth grade, Raveendran moved to S.N. College, Kannur, for a pre-university course.

Growing up in an average Malayali household in a nondescript village, Raveendran's upbringing was remarkably unremarkable. Only two things stood out from those days. First, his habit of questioning everything under the sun and trying to find the answers to all his questions through maths – he would count everything that was possibly countable.

'I remember sitting in a train and predicting its speed by counting the number of electric poles we had crossed in a certain time,' he told interviewers during a 2016 case study by Harvard Business School.

Second was his love for sports. From the very beginning, Raveendran was an outdoorsy child. He preferred the sports ground to the classroom and bunked classes so much that teachers often complained to their colleagues, his parents. To their credit, they never stopped him from playing around.

He played every sport – table tennis, cricket, football, you name it – that the school had to offer and learnt many life skills while doing so. One example Raveendran often gives is that he learnt spoken English by listening to sports commentary on the radio. He is a naturally speedy talker (as most speakers of the polysyllabic Malayalam tend to be) but his rapid-fire delivery of English was probably influenced by this as well.

Sports also taught him, in his own words, teamwork, concentration, controlled aggression, and the ability to stay calm and perform under pressure. He never worried about his studies or grades. It helped that Raveendran was a good student even if not the most punctual.

Like most middle-class people growing up in the 1980s and 1990s, Raveendran had two choices of profession to pursue after school. He could either be a doctor or an engineer. His parents wanted him to be a doctor, but Raveendran chose engineering because of how little time medical students were left with to do anything else, and he knew he couldn't not play sports. He studied mechanical engineering at Government Engineering College, Kannur, graduated in 2000 and joined a shipping firm as a service engineer in 2001.

His life changed two years later. While he was spending a vacation back home, a bunch of friends got in touch and sought Raveendran's help in preparing for the Common Admissions Test (CAT), the entrance exams for the elite Indian Institutes of Management (IIMs). These friends convinced him to take the test as well. Four out of the twelve friends cleared CAT that year, and Raveendran, as the story goes, scored a perfect 100 percentile, got calls from IIMs, cracked interviews, received joining offers, declined them, and went back to work as a service engineer with the UK-based shipping company, Pan Ocean. This, he often says, was because he never wanted to do an MBA and wrote the test for fun. He did this again in 2005 – scored a perfect 100 percentile in CAT and once again declined joining offers from IIMs. This story has been repeated so many times that it has become part of the Byju's legend. Everyone knows it but no one can check for veracity. I tried to verify Raveendran's CAT results for weeks before giving up.

After this, requests started pouring in from friends, their friends, even their friends and so on. Raveendran started offering formal classes and by the sixth or the seventh session, there were more than 1,000 students lined up for classes. Raveendran realized for the first time that he actually liked doing this and it was what he wanted to do for the rest of his life, but he still didn't want to go all in. He told his father he would do it for six months and see where it was headed. His parents have never questioned Raveendran, not when he bunked school to play sports, or when he decided against joining IIM, or when he decided to quit his globetrotting job in 2005 to teach.

Students gathered to learn from the 'CAT topper' and as his following grew, Raveendran formally started Byju's Classes for CAT in 2006. He outgrew the classroom very soon and then started holding sessions in auditoriums with class sizes of 1,200 students.

The classes were designed on a freemium model. The first class would be free and students were charged the equivalent of \$15 (around ₹750 at the time) for subsequent sessions. He would do a series of four-hour-long workshops over weekends. In these, he was mostly teaching tricks that would help students predict questions and find shortcuts to answer them. This was a practical way to approach CAT since the exam consists of objective questions, which have to be solved at speed. But this way, the learning would not be limited to the exams and would help the students learn underlying concepts.

This was unheard of in the coaching business. Everyone spoke about marks. Raveendran focused on learning. Word spread about the maverick teacher and his unconventional teaching style and Byju's became a rage. Nine out of ten students who attended the first free session enrolled for the paid workshop thereafter, making the business a huge success.

The only recurring expense was the cost of booking auditoriums. Riding on his popularity, Raveendran expanded the model to four cities – Bengaluru, Chennai, Mumbai and Pune. It was during these classes that he met students like Mrinal Mohit, Pravin Prakash, Vinay M.R., Arjun Mohan,

Anita Kishore, and his future wife, Divya Gokulnath. Some of them became co-founders at Think & Learn Pvt. Ltd – Byju's parent company – and others became lateral hires who later helped him shape India's largest edtech company.

For two years between 2007 and 2009, Raveendran targeted undergraduates and expanded to five new cities. He worked round the clock to spend time in each of these nine cities every week, doing workshops in classrooms and auditoriums. He used time in transit to simplify content, making it more accessible and engaging. This was needed because the groups were large. Logistically, it was almost impossible to make these workshops interactive; students couldn't ask questions. So Raveendran had to predict every possible question and ensure he addressed them in the content. He was a one-man army.

His fame and, therefore, his operations continued to grow beyond the nine cities, which made it impossible for Raveendran to be physically present and hold classes everywhere. By now, he was also tired of working round the clock, 7 days a week, 365 days a year.

He had hit the threshold in terms of scaling physical classes. But he had only scratched the surface of the market and he realized that. There were still hundreds of thousands, even millions, of students he could and should have reached. He needed to go deeper and increase his reach further.

The only way to do this was to digitize the content – Raveendran decided to expand through video lectures. In 2009, he started recording lectures using VSAT technology to stream videos to students across 45 cities. VSAT, or Very Small Aperture Terminal (VSAT), is a satellite-based broadcasting technology that requires minimal investment. It is used by the stock exchanges and, thus, has reached the remotest corners and gained popularity.

He managed to convince four of his brightest students to become part of his fledgling business empire. This crack team identified colleges across the country and made first contact. Where students wanted Byju's classes (which was most places), they made arrangements for the first class. These classes were taken by one of them or by Raveendran himself, and they tapped students who could take over and manage local logistics in the future. In 2010, apart from expanding his reach, Raveendran was also expanding his coverage in terms of offerings and added coaching for UPSC exams, which select aspirants for the central government services. The Byju's juggernaut was on the move and it was gaining momentum.

Raveendran is sharp and ambitious, and not just a fast talker but a fast mover, as well. When he senses an opportunity, he goes all in. It is one of the traits he picked up while playing sports. By 2011, he had tasted success and now, he wanted to go really big.

He incorporated Think & Learn Pvt. Ltd, brought in some more students as tutors and decided to expand into the school segment. The core team of Byju's students helped transform the once one-man army into a $22 billion company.

Well, them and Raveendran's younger brother Riju Ravindran. Riju is often overshadowed by his more charismatic sibling, but he was always close to the action. They were partners in crime as children, bunking school, playing cricket or sneaking off to a movie. As the company grew, Riju Ravindran kept tabs on the finances, approving all major decisions related to payments and fund allocation. His wife Deeptha A.R. led the HR vertical. She's also a low-key individual and not much is known about her outside the company.

Raveendran's wife, Divya Gokulnath, has often narrated the story of their fairy-tale relationship. After graduating in biotech from R.V. College in Bengaluru, she wanted to go overseas for higher studies and was preparing for this when she heard of the maverick teacher from one of her friends. This was 2007–08. At the class, she was awe-struck but also had a lot of questions. One thing led to another, and Raveendran convinced her to stay on after the class ended, and the two have been together since. They got married in 2009 and have two sons.

At work, Gokulnath was first a teacher. She then moved on to look after marketing and communication, mostly working from backstage. She assumed a more central role later, starting during the pandemic. As Raveendran spent more time raising funds and taking care of his sick father, she started to become the face of the company on various public forums and at media events.

Mohit became Raveendran's lieutenant, joining him in 2008. For the next decade and a half, he became the driving force behind the company's exponential growth. An electrical engineer from the Manipal Institute of Technology, he joined Byju's long before edtech had picked up pace. At the time, Mohit had been preparing for CAT and he had asked Raveendran to come to Delhi and conduct classes there. As fate would have it, Mohit became one of his earliest associates.

While all the other founders held classes when the company went online in 2015, Mohit did not. He was the quintessential sales guy. He started by orchestrating Raveendran's 'maths concerts', and would stand outside to collect the fees from attendees. From there on, he became the man responsible for raising revenue. Mohit created the relentless sales machine that pushed Byju's growth and rose through the ranks to head Byju's India operations as the COO. He would hold the fort in terms of operations while Raveendran crisscrossed the world trying to stitch together the next round of funding.

Mohit was instrumental in Byju's adoption of VSAT technology. His fingerprints are also all over the move to offline coaching centres and in the shift in the sales model to teleconferencing. Unfortunately for him, the business would ultimately outgrow him. In time, he became the scapegoat when things went sour for Byju's. In September 2023, at the time of going to press, Mohit stepped down and moved out of Byju's, handing over the reins to another former student, Arjun Mohan.

Mohan comes from Kannur but heard about 'sir' during his BTech days at the National Institute of Technology, Calicut. He took a demo class and then signed up, proceeding to crack CAT and joining IIM, Kozhikode. He would return to Byju's full-time in 2016 and rise to become the chief business officer, focusing on acquisitions and expansions.

He left in 2020, only to be back three years later as CEO of the India business.

Pravin Prakash is officially the 'chief people officer' but insiders invariably describe him as the man Friday at Byju's.

By the time Prakash heard of Raveendran, he had taken CAT a couple of times and failed. So he had mixed feelings while taking the course in Jayanagar. As luck would have it, Prakash cleared the test this time. Before the interview, however, he called 'sir' for tips. Raveendran gave him what he wanted and asked him to meet him after the IIM interview. Eventually, he convinced Prakash – who never joined IIM – to join him. He would handle infrastructure, operations and recruitment, and also double down on marketing.

Vinay M.R., another CAT aspirant, became the man behind developing content and the video format. He learnt video editing and experimented with hand motions in videos. He introduced animations.

Anita Kishore and Mohnish Jaiswal have similar stories. Kishore joined IIM Ahmedabad after cracking CAT, joined the Boston Consulting Group and then returned to the mothership as chief strategy officer. Mohit brought in Jaiswal, his junior from Manipal University. Jaiswal also handled the procurement and supply of tabs, which became a key cornerstone of the packages Byju's sold.

———

The team realized that school textbooks hadn't changed in generations and the archaic text format was not conducive to delivery over videos. They had to bring in test-prep components, like they had for the CAT and UPSC classes, to make the content more engaging for school students. So, they started playing around with textbook content, breaking it into smaller, more accessible segments and adapting it to the video format and Raveendran's unique teaching style.

'In 2012, he started a handful of offline coaching centres in Bengaluru for high school students up to grade 12 to test this product,' says a person who has worked closely with Raveendran, asking to stay anonymous. 'These centres became the playground for teachers to interact with students, take their feedback and fine-tune the product.'

Raveendran started conducting mega workshops in auditoriums for teenagers to bring them to the tuition centres. This, again, was done on a freemium model, where the first session was free and students had to pay for subsequent sessions. Like the CAT classes before them, these workshops for school students too became an instant hit. When the auditoriums became too small, Raveendran started booking stadiums. He filled New Delhi's Indira Gandhi Indoor Stadium, the country's largest indoor stadium, with more than 25,000 high school students.

But he was only getting started.

India has nearly a quarter of a billion schoolgoing students and Raveendran realized it wasn't possible to make a one-shoe-fits-all kind of product for them. He had by now disrupted the education market with his focus on learning and his unique teaching style.

But if he had to tap into this huge market, his product needed to stand tall and be sharply differentiated in the crowded offline coaching business. He had to focus on making learning more intuitive and effective. The only way to do it was to focus on individual learning experiences, and to do that the company needed to work with different experiences and experiment with multiple formats.

One insight was that each student has a different learning approach and pace. Some learn better by reading text, others by watching videos, yet others by listening to stories or by doing things themselves, and so on. In order to create maximum impact, the company needed to adopt all these different approaches, creating content in formats like written, visual and algebraic, so that the odds of students missing out on learning could be minimized. The company hired experts from various backgrounds to tweak content, and worked with a motley crew of engineers, animators, 3D designers, visual-effects specialists, even professional musicians in addition to teachers.

Byju's took the common elements from different curricula and broke down the concepts into modules lasting only around five minutes to make them accessible for students across education boards. Creating the script was the first challenge. The team identified key questions and then found suitable answers with the use of daily objects. The script then went through multiple iterations, incorporating feedback from students, and the final script was broken into second-by-second storyboards to explain the topic. This would become the platform for the final video lesson. It would often take days and even weeks to create an hour-long module.

Byju's superimposed animation to real videos to explain concepts better and increase engagement. For example, if a teacher is talking about a circle, she would move her hand in a circle and a circle will be created on the screen. Now, if she needs to make a chord in the circle or break the circle at one point to illustrate it to be a straight line, all she needs is one hand movement.

Students were already spending a lot of time on a mobile phone or a tablet to play games and watch movies, and Raveendran realized that it would be impossible to retain students unless you could match that kind of quality and content delivery.

The company used real-life scenarios to explain concepts. For example, to explain projectile motion, it used a cricket shot. It would play a short video clip of the shot, mark the motion and trajectory of the ball, and then turn it into a graphical representation. All of this is much easier said than done.

When I visited the IBC Knowledge Park office in Bengaluru in November 2022, it felt like an archipelago of many small islands, each with a set group of professionals working on different parts of the puzzle to perfect the content. In one cubicle, a group of animators kept fiddling with their computers to get the angle of a video correct. In a soundproof room in another corner, a bunch of musicians were fine-tuning a jingle. Every corner of the office was abuzz with activity.

A chance meeting with Ranjan Pai, the Manipal Group scion, in 2012 changed the course of the company. Pai was visiting his hometown Manipal in Karnataka and was staying in the Fortune Inn Valley View hotel, when one nippy winter morning during his stay, Pai noticed the hotel was brimming with students carrying notebooks, engaged in animated conversation. He checked with the manager who told him the unusual activity was because a teacher was conducting coaching classes for hundreds of CAT aspirants. His curiosity was piqued. He requested the manager to arrange a meeting and the manager obliged. The next morning, Pai met Raveendran over coffee.

Pai heard the younger man talk about his humble beginnings and the business, and asked if he needed money to grow. He also suggested that if Raveendran wanted to scale his business, he should consider going digital. The offline model might not be scalable. Then, he offered to invest if Raveendran wanted to take Byju's online.

Raveendran sought time to think things over. Days passed. Then a week. Around 10 days later, he came back with a proposal, asking Pai to invest ₹50 crore in the business. This was almost 10 times the amount Pai had had in mind for Byju's. Still, he let Raveendran explain things. As things turned out, Pai decided to invest the proposed amount in several tranches and, in 2013, Pai's Aarin Capital became Byju's first investor. In exchange, it got a 26% stake in Byju's, which Aarin Capital sold a few years down the line, making more than 10x return on its investment.

Byju's went into incubation and, in 2015, the company launched Byju's The Learning App. By now, it had built-in content for multiple grades, and the company was getting even more deeply involved with schooling, moving down from board exam aspirants all the way to kindergarten.

In addition to its product, the app was offering a personal mentor to support students and guide them through their learning journey. The first modules offered maths and science programmes for grades eight through twelve and also material for competitive exams like CAT, UPSC and GMAT.

The company developed two versions of each course. One was an online streaming version and the other was delivered on a memory card (SD card) preloaded with content. This was bundled with Samsung or Lenovo tablets and given to subscribers. The SD card version worked better for smaller centres and small towns with low/slow internet connectivity. The sale of these SD cards would grow to become the company's single biggest revenue stream in the future, but we will come to that later.

The app also stuck to the tried-and-tested freemium model. Once a user downloaded the app, they could use the content free for a few weeks and then they had the option to pay an annual subscription fee equivalent to around $150 to unlock more content.

Byju's went to town with advertising campaigns and targeted social media campaigns. It employed hundreds of foot soldiers to convert people who downloaded the apps into paid subscribers. This salesforce would become the biggest growth engine for the company and also one of the key reasons behind its undoing. But again, let's not get ahead of ourselves.

In June 2015, the company raised a $25 million investment

Mark Zuckerberg ✓
September 8, 2016 · 🌐

      ···

As part of the Chan Zuckerberg Initiative, Priscilla and I are investing in an Indian education technology company we're excited about called BYJU's.

BYJU's was started by a teacher and entrepreneur named Byju Raveendran as a way to help students from different backgrounds across India learn in a way that works best for them. The mobile app uses a mix of video lessons and interactive tools to help teach subjects like math and science for a fraction of what other services cost. So far, BYJU's has 250,000 subscribers who use the app for an average of 40 minutes a day -- and it's working. A survey found that almost 80 percent of parents said it improved their children's learning dramatically.

I'm optimistic about personalized learning and the difference it can make for students everywhere. That's why it's a major focus of our education efforts, and why we're looking forward to working with companies like BYJU's to get these tools into the hands of more students and teachers around the world.

🔵 Bhuvaneshwari Natarajan and 109K others   6.2K comments   10K shares

👍 Like   💬 Comment   ↪ Share

*Mark Zuckerberg mentioned this investment in a Facebook post,
which went viral.*

from Sequoia Capital India (which was rebranded as Peak XV Ventures in 2023). The company doubled down on its growth strategy and by December that year, app downloads and conversions had exceeded expectations.

In the middle of the next year, it raised another $50 million from the Chan Zuckerberg Initiative.

Mark Zuckerberg mentioned this investment in a Facebook post, which went viral.

Growth in Byju's exploded. By September 2016, the company had over 2,000 people on the rolls. The Learning App had been downloaded more than 7 million times and there were around 300,000 paid users. The rest, as they say, is history.

2

The Great Indian Rat Race

The first time my mother found me reading a comic book, she freaked out. This was in the early 1990s. She took away the comic book, gave me a good beating, and threatened to do worse. When my father returned from work that evening, a family meeting was called. The parents told me I shouldn't waste my time reading junk and should instead focus on academics if I wanted a better life. The pre-teen me couldn't understand any of it. What did comic books have to do with a better life?

Over the years, however, I've come to understand where my parents were coming from and I've chosen to forgive and forget because their attitude mirrors that of so many Indian parents from low-income, hard-scrabble backgrounds. My parents and many like them were classic Byju's 'leads' or 'targets' in sales-speak, but of course, there was no Byju's back then.

Not much has changed in terms of attitudes. An education expert, 'Anita' (name changed to protect identity) once told me circa 2020, 'Parents will happily give away a kidney and a limb in exchange for better education for children, because that is the only way to break social and economic barriers.'

My parents were both refugees from a war-torn country – erstwhile East Pakistan, now Bangladesh. They were both school dropouts and came to Bihar sometime in the 1970s. They had difficult lives, to put it mildly.

Mother's family settled in a small village some 15 km from Bettiah in West Champaran district. My grandmother, a widow, didn't have a job or any other means of income to take care of her five children, so it was all hands on deck when it came to finding odd jobs to help run the household. They did all sorts of things, from working on the local farms to making bidis.

My late father – peace be upon him – left the war in Bangladesh behind and moved to Krishnanagar in the Nadia district of West Bengal. Then he moved to Patna in search of a job. It was a strange city. He didn't know a word of Hindi and didn't venture out for days until hunger took over. He often told me and my sister the story of how he came to an unknown city, with only ₹2, a pair of clothes and slippers. He slept on the floor on a jute bag and covered himself with another bag during the harsh winter months.

How they met and then stitched together a life for us is an incredible story in itself. But I digress. My sister and I used to hear these stories often, usually narrated to us as pointed moral science lessons, especially when our parents thought we weren't focusing enough on our studies. If only they had had the luxury of education, my parents thought, they could have had a better life and given us a better upbringing. So, it was essential that we spent all our time studying. They found a private tutor for us. I even went to a coaching centre to prepare for entrance exams for medical studies. Because my parents didn't know better, they left us to the care of the teachers and the coaching centres. As they saw it, doing well academically was our only shot at improving our condition – the only bridge to a better future.

Three decades later, things haven't changed much for many lower-income families. Parents still work themselves to the bone to ensure they can give their children a push up the educational ladder. They scrape up the financial resources, and employ everything from physical coercion to emotional blackmail to induce their children to study. The new digital options – apps like Byju's – and the online learning tools created by education technology have just added more alternatives and options and amplified FOMO for anxious parents.

———

Cut to June 2023. Naveen sounded apologetic over the phone. He was my regular auto guy when I lived in Delhi and used to go to the office. It had been a while and I had called him to catch up. He told me he had slapped his 11-year-old son for the first time because he didn't know how else to get through to the young boy.

'*Main thak gaya hoon, bhaiya. Usko samajh hi nahi aata. School mein padhai nahi hoti, to tuition lagwaya tha. Do din se tuition nahi ja raha. Ghar se nikalta hai aur doston ke saath khelne chala jata hai. Teacher ne kal phone kiya to pata chala*' (I am tired. He doesn't understand. He doesn't learn much in school, so I got him a tutor. But he hasn't been there for two days now. He goes out playing instead. We got to know after the tutor called yesterday), he said. '*Padhega nahi to kya karega? Baap ki tarah auto chalayega?*' (If he doesn't study hard, what will he do? Drive an autorickshaw like his father?)

Naveen, 38, lives in Burari in northeast Delhi with his wife and three children. Like his homemaker wife, he is also a school dropout and, thus, the couple learned about the value of education the hard way. Until the lockdown, they used to send their children to a private, English-medium school. In addition, the children also had a private tutor who came home. But the lockdown was brutal. Naveen's income evaporated as autorickshaws stopped plying. The family moved into a smaller house and cut down on all expenses, but they still could not afford a private school.

Post-lockdown, after paying for the fuel and the daily rent for the autorickshaw, Naveen makes about ₹500–700 on a good day. Some days, even that is a stretch. His children now go to government-run schools.

'*Tuition ka kharcha bhi mushkil se nikalta hai. Kabhi sochta hoon band kar doon. Fir lagta hai, bachchon ko padhana zaroori hai. Ajkal competition itna ho gaya hai, ki tuition ke bina kaam nahi chalta. To kisi tarah kar raha hoon*' (We can hardly afford the tuition. Sometimes, I think about stopping it. But then education is important. With competition getting tougher, they won't be able to do without tuitions. So, I am managing somehow), he said.

'*Bachchon ki zindagi ban jaaye bas. Hamari tarah na rahein. Aur kya chahiye.*' (I want the children to have a better life and not be like us. That's all.)

I've heard that refrain time and again while talking to leads, as the salespeople refer to potential signups.

———

Professor Ashoka Mody writes in his brilliant *India Is Broken* that successive governments since 1947 have failed to lift the vast majority of the population above the state of despair. For example, every government promises job creation. Yet, unemployment is still hovering around the 8% mark in mid-2023 as I write this.

Education, therefore, is seen as the key, perhaps the only key, to a better standard of living and a relatively more prosperous future. It is a means to an end. Most Indians study not to become free thinkers or for the love of learning, but just to get a job, any job. Anything that brings in a steady income and helps alleviate the pain and suffering of growing up in poverty.

After every round of competitive exams, the front pages of newspapers and the TV channels are littered with the stories of toppers who came from humble backgrounds – every one of those interviewees explains how they want to transform the lives of their parents who have sacrificed everything so that their children could get ahead in life.

Readers find collective joy in celebrating these stories because most of us have also been part of this system. We know how difficult it is to rise against all odds and how much the Indian system is rigged against the have-nots.

The basic problem is that India's public education system is broken. Here, too, successive governments at the Centre and states have failed the people.

Note that I am not even referring to the fact that our education and its syllabi are obsolete. The British aimed to produce clerks, who could take orders and follow commands. The world has moved on since. But India's education system? Not quite so much. Much of what we learn in school doesn't have any practical application in our lives.

India has one of the world's largest school education systems with around 265 million children enrolled in pre-primary to higher-secondary level across 1.5 million schools, according to the government's UDISE+ Report for 2020–21.

But the physical infrastructure is poor and the less said about the quality of education imparted the better. A large number of government-run schools lack basic infrastructure such as classrooms, toilets, and clean drinking water. Around 25% of teachers are absent on any given day. To improve the student–teacher ratio, at least on paper, the government started recruiting untrained teachers at lesser pay. But that has widened the learning gap. One has to only look at the Annual Status of Education Report (ASER) over the years to realize that most school children struggle with the 3Rs of education – Reading, wRiting, and aRithmetic.

The ASER is prepared by NGO Pratham on the basis of household surveys conducted across 616 rural districts and it covers 6,90,000 children between the ages of 3 and 16. The latest report, ASER 2022, was released in January 2023. It shows that only one in five children in grade 3 could read grade 2-level texts.

That report came out after four years and it took into account the impact of lockdown during the Covid-19 pandemic. But it is not like the pre-pandemic situation was much better. In 2018, for example, only one in four students in grade 3 could read grade 2-level text, according to ASER 2022. The percentage of children in grade 5 who could read grade 2-level text fell to 42.8% in 2022 from 50.5% in 2018. More than 56% of grade 8 children couldn't do division.

A similar report isn't available for students in government-run schools in cities, but anecdotal evidence and the high failure rates of students from government schools in board exams suggests they aren't doing much better. So, there is a general migration towards private schools, which make up nearly 25% of total schools in India and account for nearly 45% of India's schoolgoing population – and this number is rising – according to the 'State of the Sector Report: Private Schools in India' by Central Square Foundation, a non-profit organization working in the education sector.

The inefficiencies of the school education system, combined with high-pressure exams, have led to the proliferation of a huge after-school, or supplementary education, industry. There is also a social angle to this.

There's always been a willingness to invest in children's futures, but the rise in nuclear families, sometimes with both parents out working, has led to a lack of time and lack of support from the community. Often, parents also lack the time and ability to guide their children academically. Hence, they are left with no choice other than to send their children to private tuitions or coaching centres.

The concept of supplementary education is neither new nor novel. It has been gaining popularity even in advanced industrial economies and developing countries, across economic classes and political and cultural contexts, for decades.

There was a time when this after-school-study segment was seen as a temporary solution. It started with individual tutors working from home but now it has evolved into a multi-billion dollar business. The market size of India's coaching classes is expected to reach more than $19 billion by 2030, according to Pune-based consultancy Infinium Research.

An estimated 71 million children, nearly one in four school students, attended private tuitions or coaching classes, according to the National Sample Survey 2016. 'Edtech in India: A Turning Point', an Omidyar Network India and RedSeer report published in 2020, estimates this number to be closer to 90 million, suggesting one in three schoolchildren uses supplementary education.

'This wouldn't be the case if our schools had better facilities and teachers. Teachers also hardly have any time and bandwidth left after admin tasks like paperwork, corrections, etc. It is a systemic failure,' an academic and education expert told me during an interview.

Teachers also find tuition classes or coaching centres more lucrative because they not only offer more money and autonomy, but also rid them of tedious clerical work.

But your friendly neighbourhood teacher and the big coaching chains and everyone in between is feeding off the combination of two things. First, there's the flawed education system. And second, the constant parental urge to provide children with the best education, and the perpetual paranoia and guilt associated with it. It is the same story across every village and city.

Coaching hubs like Kota just cashed in on this combination of a broken education system and desperate parents trying to give their children a shot at a better future. As did Byju's.

———

Vinod Kumar Bansal, a freshly minted mechanical engineer from Banaras Hindu University (now IIT BHU), landed in the industrial city of Kota in Rajasthan, around 240 km from the capital Jaipur, in 1971, with a job at JK Synthetics. But a few years into the job, he was diagnosed with muscular dystrophy, a hereditary muscle disease for which there is no cure. It killed his dream to become a chief engineer. As the disease worsened and restricted his movements, Bansal was unable to keep up with his day job.

He was already helping neighbourhood students prepare for entrance tests for engineering courses, and as his disease progressed, Bansal decided to pursue this part-time hobby in a more meaningful way. In the early 1980s, he started teaching eight students sitting around his dining table. In 1983, when his company shut down, Bansal started teaching full-time. Some of his students got into the IITs and word spread that 'Bansal sir' had a magic touch. Soon, parents in Kota, and then from outside Rajasthan, sought his help. In 1991, Bansal Classes was born.

Soon enough, students flocked to Kota from all parts of India. Bansal Classes became a rage, and imitators sprang up. As students poured into the little Rajasthani town, hostels, tiffin centres and other logistics developed to service these teenagers. The city transformed from a sleepy industrial small town into India's coaching capital as a tsunami of coaching centres took over the landscape.

Today, there are more than 150 coaching institutes in Kota, catering to around 2,00,000 students aspiring to get into elite engineering and medical colleges in the country. The city is considered a Mecca for engineering hopefuls whose main focus is to secure a seat in one of the Indian Institutes of Technology.

Here's the catch, though. In 2023, according to Professor Bishnupada Mandal, organizing chairperson of the Joint Entrance Exams (JEE Advanced) 2023, there were 17,385 seats across the 23 IITs and more than 1.1 million students competing for them. Those who can't secure a seat in IITs have to settle for other less elite engineering colleges.

But Kota gives you a better shot than most. Every year, tens of thousands of students from Kota's coaching centres clear the JEE Mains exams. In 2023, four students from Kota made it to the top 10 ranks.

It is not surprising then that these coaching institutes wear all-India rankings (AIR) as a badge of honour. Equally unsurprising is the fact that many of these institutes have an internal selection process, including an entrance test, to ensure their own quality of intake. The competition, and the fear of missing out (FOMO), is fierce. Under the circumstances, anyone making a tonic to help a child's memory will make a killing. The places of worship in Kota receive huge donations every year from grateful and hopeful parents.

The education technology companies took it to yet another level when it came to exploiting this FOMO.

———

When Byju's launched its Learning App in 2015, it started by offering programmes in maths and science for students from grades 8 to 12 and programmes for CAT, UPSC and GMAT.

The pitch was that because there was so much focus on exams and marks, students forgot the art of learning, and the sheer fun associated with it. Memorizing and regurgitating in exams was, and still is, the norm. But Byju's said that by making children learn concepts as early as grade 8, it would make them future-ready for IITs and IIMs. Over the years, the company has kept launching programmes for even younger children and it has pushed the 'sooner-you-start-the-better-the-odds-your-child-has-at-clearing-IIT/IIM/NEET' pitch to their parents.

This 'catch them young and make them future-ready' strategy was also milked by companies like WhiteHat Jr and Clever Harvey. WhiteHat Jr claimed that the future belonged to the creators. 'Any job that doesn't involve a level of creation will be automated,' was founder Karan Bajaj's favourite line to say in media interactions. The company launched courses that taught coding to children as young as six. It also went berserk with advertisements that depicted a fictional 9-year-old 'Wolf Gupta' earning a 10-figure salary by coding at a global tech conglomerate.

If this wasn't enough, Clever Harvey took it a notch

further by launching 15-hour 'junior MBA' courses for teenagers. Edtech offerings during the pandemic became so absurd that it became difficult to tell the difference between a fact and a meme.

In the initial years at Byju's, the focus was on making sales and getting business. The company hired young graduates from engineering schools and deployed them in telecalling. These callers would introduce themselves as IIT graduates and talk to parents about the future of their children.

'This was 2016, and we could do anything to make the sale,' one former employee, 'Amit' (the name has been changed on request), who had joined the company as an intern in 2016 and rose through the ranks to become a manager, told me. 'No one was monitoring the calls and it was a free pass. We just had to make the numbers.'

Managers, at least those in Bengaluru, were given a weekly party budget and were encouraged to take the team out once a week and bond over drinks.

'The real job of the managers started after 10 p.m. on our weekends. They would take us out for drinks, figure out the people with the best numbers and manipulate them to stick around, and do even better,' Amit said.

Often the young telemarketers would say they wanted to pursue higher studies. Their managers would tell them that this was a futile ambition. Their logic: eventually a higher degree would help somebody get a job somewhere in some company where they would have to start again from scratch. At Byju's, in comparison, they were equal stakeholders. The 'vibe', the autonomy they got at Byju's, was something they wouldn't get anywhere else. Plus, instead of taking time off to study, if they stuck around with Byju's, they would make better money and climb up the corporate ladder faster.

Interns were given examples of other employees who had cracked the sales code and made it big. 'It was like those motivational speeches at the MLM (multi-level marketing) companies where they tell you how XYZ made it big and how you can do the same,' said Amit.

'Managers manipulated these interns who, in turn, would manipulate parents so they would end up buying the product. Exploiting FOMO would be the starting point. They would end up shaming and threatening the parents till they submitted and signed up their children.'

3

The Art of Selling

₹18,000.

That was all that stood between the child's present circumstances living in a Mumbai chawl and his parents' hopes of a better future. It would be an investment – a bridge to the wider and more prosperous world beyond the chawl.

The parents desperately wanted to give their child a shot at a better education, something they had never had. They would have happily sacrificed everything for that. Yet, despite all their efforts, all they could arrange was ₹1,500. The bridge to the future was crumbling.

So, when they found out that they could take a loan for the rest of the amount, their happiness knew no bounds. In that moment, they were happier than Charlie during his first visit to the chocolate factory.

The salesperson from Maharashtra who told me this story remembered that breezy day around December 2018 like it was yesterday. 'Bobby' (name changed) requested anonymity. He was following a lead given to him earlier that week by the team in Bengaluru. As a BDE, or business development executive, with Byju's, his job was to convert that lead into a sale of The Learning App.

As his cab approached the address, though, his heart started sinking. GPS led him to a chawl, where he knew that a sale would be close to impossible. But he needed this one to complete his targets. In his short stint at Byju's, his numbers had been fine. He didn't want to botch this one up. Not now, in his final few days at the company.

'The parents were extremely vulnerable. To be honest, every parent is,' Bobby told me over the phone. 'But that set of parents, their eyes, I can't forget them. They told me, "We want to do something for the child; we want to give him what we didn't have, but we can't even afford simple things."'

He told them about The Learning App and how it could help their child in his education. He also told them about the option of taking a loan from Capital Float, one of Byju's lending partners at the time. An hour into the meeting, he finally made what he remembered as his most desperate sale. 'I had a feeling that I would get a refund call soon from the parents,' he said.

Things hadn't felt right.

First, the child went to a government school where English was not the medium of teaching. His command over the language, which Byju's used for all its lessons, was much below par.

Second, he was a slow learner, a fact that Bobby had gathered from his interaction with the child. Letting children learn at their own pace can only go so far. Frustration creeps in with each wrong answer.

As the BDE expected, the father called and asked for a

refund, which was done promptly. But in hindsight, the BDE says, he shouldn't have sold to those parents in the first place.

But not all such meetings – called counselling calls – are morally ambiguous in the same way. Bobby also recalls the time he sold a package to a couple for their children within 10 minutes. In contrast to the parents in the chawl, those parents were well-informed and affluent. They requested a demo and immediately cut a cheque for ₹1.5 lakh (~$2,000) for a four-year course for their two children in grade 6. No convincing or explanation was required.

'The ticket value of that deal should have been ₹1.2 lakh (~$1,600),' Bobby said. 'But I overpitched and they bought it at ₹1.5 lakh without any questions.'

———

Did you read the two stories above? Read them again. Slowly, this time.

Over the last 45 months, as I reported on education technology for The Morning Context, I have heard more than a hundred stories from Byju's salespeople about their lives, work and sales tactics. But this salesperson's account stands out for the sheer contrasts.

It presents two sets of parents, one from each end of the socio-economic spectrum, both wanting what is best for their children, and the salesperson playing fast and loose in different ways with both sets to make the sale. The moral dilemma was different in both cases.

Since it launched its Learning App in 2015, Byju's has revolutionized learning. It must be given credit for the big changes it has wrought. For the first time in the history of India's education system, someone was talking about learning and not marks. It was unbelievable and heartwarming at the same time. Byju's preached that the ultimate goal of all education is learning. It is not about being robots, memorizing and regurgitating results, but instead about learning concepts and their application where required. Learning remains at the heart of Byju's operations, at least on paper.

But for the learning to happen, and for the company to make a sustainable business on the back of that desire to learn, the app needed to reach a large number of people.

Selling the app to parents was a challenge and parents are the final arbiters and decision makers in the kindergarten to grade 12 segment where Byju's was operating. This contrasts with the test-prep or higher education segment, where the student looks for options and often takes the final call. So, the kindergarten to grade 12 segment of edtech runs on push sales, unlike the other segments that rely on the brand's image and pull sales.

Sometime during the latter half of 2015, the company launched an advertisement blitz across TV as well as digital campaigns on social media. The first task was to get the students or their parents to download the app. The ads on TV and social media campaigns were good and had plenty of recall value, but Byju's needed a bigger dhamaka (blast). It also had to keep its target audience in mind – children, the end-users, and parents, the buyers.

Only two things in India cut through all societal boundaries, Raveendran told me once: cricket and Bollywood.

So, when Byju's needed mass appeal, something to make the company a household name, he acted upon that insight.

On Children's Day (14 November) in 2017, Byju's launched one of the biggest and most popular ad campaigns of all time, starring none other than Bollywood superstar Shah Rukh Khan. Created by Lowe Lintas, the ad shows Khan with a group of children during a school's annual day performance. Here's what Raveendran said in a media release announcing the collaboration with Khan:

Children rarely use the word 'Love' and 'Learning' together as learning has always been equated to pressure, stress and competition. We have always strongly believed that children learn better when they love what they learn. Our partnership with Shah Rukh Khan will help us increase our reach and create a deeper connect across geographies. His wide appeal and adoration amongst parents and children makes him a perfect fit for our brand.

Barring a brief hiatus in 2021, when Khan's son was arrested, Byju's association with him continues till today.

Raveendran hadn't forgotten about cricket either. Nearly two years later, in July 2019, just ahead of the ICC Men's Cricket World Cup, the edtech company replaced mobile handset maker Oppo as the Indian cricket team's main sponsor.

'We are proud to be the Indian cricket team sponsor. Cricket is the heartbeat of all Indians and we are thrilled to be an integral part of our much-loved team,' Raveendran said in a statement. 'As a learning company, Byju's has always recognized the critical role that sport plays in a child's development. Just as cricket inspires a billion budding dreams across India, we too as a learning company hope to inspire the love of learning in every child's heart.'

One week later, COO Mrinal Mohit told Adgully, a media platform for advertising and marketing, that the company would spend 15% of the marketing budget on the ICC Cricket World Cup 2019.

Here's what Mohit said to Adgully: 'Our product is visual and we want the parents to understand how early learning will make their children better learners for life in about 30 seconds. Advertising on TV has always helped us with customer acquisition, that is, increased downloads. From the time we launch, we measure the ROI [Return on Investment] of our ad campaigns, through downloads, subscriptions, etc. We are very paranoid about the performance of an ad; if we see it performing well, we are ready to invest. In terms of mediums, we have seen that TV, when used simultaneously with social media, amplifies our ROI.'

As the company grew further and looked outside India for its expansion, it needed a global face – somebody who could replicate the Khan effect. It needed a sport with the same fanatical following across the world as cricket has in India – somebody and something to work the same magic as cricket and Bollywood.

There was only one possible sport and only one individual. In March 2022, the company announced it had signed up as an official sponsor of the FIFA World Cup Football, which was scheduled to be held later that year in Qatar.

In November 2022, Byju's announced Lionel Messi would

be the first global brand ambassador of its social impact arm, Education For All. The announcement coincided more or less with mass layoffs in the company and, thus, created a lot of furore in mainstream media as well as social media.

But the goal was to become a household name across the world and what better way than signing up Messi? The high-power collaboration would send brand recall into the stratosphere. So, Byju's spared no expense.

The company's advertisement and promotion expenses grew from ₹188 crore in FY18 to ₹457 crore in FY19, to ₹899 crore in FY20, and an eye-popping ₹2,251 crore in FY21, according to its audited earnings reports. Byju's topline – consolidated revenue for FY21 – amounted to ₹2,428 crore, so A&P expense was a whopping 92.7% of revenue in FY21.

But generating brand recall and getting people to download the app was only the first step in turning that download into revenue. The moment somebody downloads the app and signs up with their contact details, they become a 'lead'. Mohit told me in 2020 that the company reaches out to children who have used the app for more than 15 days. But salespeople tell me the company doesn't actually wait that long. Their usage is monitored over a few days and their number is given to a salesperson to follow up. Each salesperson gets around 30–50 such leads daily. The idea is to convert a lead into, first, a counselling session, and then a sale.

When I downloaded the app in February 2020, Byju's got in touch within a week and the telemarketing call was interesting. I had downloaded the Byju's app, played two videos and taken one quiz. On the fifth day after downloading the app, I got a call from the company.

Caller: Your number has been shortlisted for Byju's special scholarship programme. We're running a campaign in Delhi–NCR wherein we have shortlisted some students based on the activity on the application.

Me: How much is the scholarship?

Caller: It is 50%, but it also depends on the course you buy and the duration.

Me: Tell me about the three-year course from grade four to six.

Caller: You will have to pay ₹2,500–3,000 per month for 12 months. But it may vary, depending upon the assessment by our senior counsellor who will visit your home. On Byju's website, separate courses for the three grades are available for ₹30,000 each year.

Me: How many students do you give such scholarships to?

Caller: I can't give you a number for pan-India. But in Delhi–NCR, we only give such scholarships to about 200 students. We can't give more because we have to provide personalized support to them.

Me: So, you don't give personalized mentoring support to every child who buys?

Caller: No. We don't have the manpower for it. The personalized support is only for those students who avail of the scholarship in this season.

Me: How many scholarship seasons do you have in a year? Does it go on through the year?

Caller: No, it doesn't. But the number depends on top management.

I hung up. I kept getting calls from that and other numbers, as well as messages, congratulating me on winning the scholarship and nudging me to buy a course for several months.

Converting people who download the app into paid subscribers was, and still is, the number one challenge for Byju's. The buyer of the product, the parent, is different from the user, the child. The sales team has to convince the buyer that the app would actually help the user, and this means hard-selling the app to the buyer, while more delicately convincing the user it would be useful.

There are other challenges too. First, in India at least, the efficacy of education is measured by the number of marks scored in an exam. So convincing parents about the utility of an app that focuses on learning and doesn't guarantee higher marks is a herculean task. This is even more difficult since there are plenty of options that claim to help students memorize concepts and score higher in exams.

The high, one-time investment in an untested product is also another reason for buyer resistance. So, the idea was to make parents believe in learning more than in memorizing and somehow earn their trust.

The task, as both Raveendran and Mohit explained to me in different conversations, was to explain to parents how The Learning App was made and how it could help their children start learning better compared with all the other modes of supplementary education.

Byju's created a sales team of fresh engineering graduates from all over India to get this job done. Why only engineering graduates, you might ask? Because maths is at the heart of

The Learning App. And to sell the app, the company needed smart individuals who not only understood those concepts but could also make others understand them in quick, informal interactions.

Naturally, the selection process for the sales team, at least in the beginning, was rigorous. Mohit told me during our interaction that the company used to get thousands of job applications and selected only about 10% of the people for sales roles. Over the years, the initial 300-member team grew to thousands of foot soldiers working in the field, chasing leads and targets, scouting for parents whose varied circumstances might oscillate anywhere between the two extreme situations mentioned above, where one set of parents paid ₹1.5 lakh without blinking, while the other struggled to pay ₹18,000.

Learning may indeed be at the heart of Byju's operation, but sales is indisputably the oxygen for the organization. If there is one thing the company has been able to crack, it is the sales-driven growth model. However unsustainable this might have proved in hindsight, it was the sales strategy that turned Byju's into India's largest edtech company.

Remember, that the focus is supposed to be on explaining and making parents trust the product. In reality, here's how the sales machinery works as I learnt from interactions with many salespeople and parents.

Round after persistent round of cold calling begins once the sales team gets into the act. It is often worse than credit card calls, almost bordering on harassment. I have heard recordings of some of these cold calls in which the parent, frustrated by the insistent calls, unleashed the choicest abuse on the salesperson and threatened them with police complaints. But once a parent engages, the game is on.

Over the phone call, the salesperson tries to understand the parents' level of involvement with the child's studies. Then they throw in a deal – say, a 50% scholarship – as bait. Indians are value-conscious, but they also love discounts and a 'scholarship' sounds prestigious. So, in edtech jargon a discount is a 'scholarship', and they are offered all the time. Without exceptions. Many parents bite, though salespeople say the conversion ratio is less than one sale for every 10 downloads.

A counselling session is scheduled. Most such meetings happen over the weekend or after 7 p.m. between Wednesdays and Fridays. That's when both parents are generally home. In 90% of the cases where the second parent is not home, salespeople say the sale doesn't go through. These sessions can last anywhere between 15 minutes and a couple of hours, depending on factors like affordability, involvement with the child's education, and the parents' general awareness of the app and of education. Remember the two sets of parents we talked about earlier?

Salespeople have told me that they constantly look for clues that may help them understand the spending capacity of the parents: the location of the home, the size of the television, everything becomes a visual clue. They talk to the child about their interests and ambitions, and try to create a rapport. Then they move into the next stage of trying to close the deal.

The salesperson asks some questions on a certain subject/ topic or gives a quiz. The salesperson has to prove to the parents that the child's learning lacks direction before suggesting that Byju's is the solution. Roughly 20 sets of parents have told me over the last three years that they feel demotivated, embarrassed and guilty that they have not been able to do enough for their children.

One of the most popular questions these salespeople ask children in grades 6 and above is about the total number of points on a circle. Most children fail to answer that question. Then, the salesperson explains that a circle has an infinite number of points. To make parents understand the simplicity of the concept, they show them Raveendran's introduction to geometry video.

A simple question follows, exploiting the parents' guilt and FOMO: if the child can't learn the fundamentals, how will they do well in the tenth grade board exams and onwards?

Then the salesperson sweetens the offer by offering a 'scholarship', which is what advertising professionals would describe as a discount on the 'rack rate'. Earlier, Byju's used to include a personal mentor for the child but that service has since stopped.

At this point, most children would want the tablet. (Byju's used to collaborate with tech companies such as Samsung and Lenovo to create customized learning kits that included a tablet preloaded with learning material from the company. In early 2023, as it suffered a cash-crunch, it stopped bundling these tablets.)

By now, the parents are emotional and worried about their child's future education if the sales pitch has been delivered effectively. The smartly dressed salesperson then asks the parents to give it a try with the reassuring statement that if you don't like it, you can get a full refund. Most parents are close to giving in by now. This is the time for one final blow.

The salesperson then throws several other questions at the child, planned so that the child will fail to answer. These questions might seem almost random but they are not. They are parts of the topics covered in the videos that the salesperson proceeds to show next. After the videos, the questions are repeated, and this time, the child answers correctly. It is a trick that never fails. The parents are satisfied. A deal is struck.

Clinching a sale is not about the child. It is about exploiting the fear of the parents regarding the child's future in a broken education system. It is about convincing them about the efficacy of Byju's Learning App. And a skilled salesperson will change the tone of the conversation from persuasion to intimidation to shaming the parents for not caring enough about their child's future.

Mohit told me that onboarding parents wasn't very difficult, and sales targets weren't very stiff – 'It was difficult when we launched in 2015 . . . I used to make a hundred calls a day. Those were difficult times,' he told me. He also said that salespeople can't promise a 50% scholarship. But my personal experience and the stories I have heard from salespeople and parents are at odds with his assertions.

———

Let's take a step back from the anecdotal to understand how

this business model evolved. The supplementary education market picked up pace because our education system failed students for generations. But as more students relied on tuition and coaching centres, these also started facing the same problems that India's schools did – too many students, not enough infrastructure, demotivated teachers.

New-age education companies, powered by tech, promised to solve these problems. But eventually, pressures created by the need to grow kicked in there as well. To maximize revenue, edtech companies started locking parents into multi-year deals. Lenders chipped in with easy EMI solutions where parents couldn't pay the total cost of the product upfront.

This has now led to a serious debt trap.

And this is how it worked.

On the day of the home visit, the salesperson would try to get the parents to sign up, by whatever means necessary. They told me that they can't come back empty-handed. So, they would cut whatever deal they deemed possible.

Finally, the salesperson would ask for PAN and Aadhaar numbers and bank details, generate one-time passwords, and assure parents that EMIs would start flowing after several weeks and that they had the option of cancelling before that happens. They would all then pose for happy selfies with the child.

Then all hell would break loose.

Parents would realize that the product didn't live up to the promises. They would keep going around in circles, trying to return the product and cancel the subscription. But by then, the loan would have been approved, the EMIs would kick in and the return window would close. If the parents didn't pay, their credit score would get affected and the lender would start making threatening calls. Crucially, unlike the neighbourhood tutor or coaching centre that they could leave because there were no long-term commitments, they would wander around lost in the edtech chakravyuha (trap).

Not all refund requests are declined, though. Many customers have got their money back but only after a long and trying process. The best way to get the refunds, according to multiple salespeople, was and still is to take the complaints to social media. All such complaints on social media that got traction were resolved quickly. But the number of people seeking refunds hasn't declined.

Raveendran & Co. deny that there are many refunds, but they have not shared any data about this and the audited accounts also obfuscate this point, making it difficult to figure out the returns ratio. Anecdotal evidence is that a large number of people are still stuck in the system, demanding refunds and not using the edtech product or services, and that number is rising by the day.

As edtech expands beyond the metro cities to small towns and villages, this problem seems to be worsening. Most parents require financing and once a third party finances the purchase, there is just no easy way to get a refund.

Here is how an edtech executive explained this issue to me:

'Edtech firms get paid in full by fintech firms. Then it becomes the fintech firm's problem. In some cases, where there is a default, the edtech and fintech firms share the losses. But in most cases, the customers ultimately end up paying, fearing either a legal mess or societal shame. Which more than recovers the overall loss for these companies.'

To understand the processes better, you have to comprehend something called the FLDG, a financial tool that created a lot of buzz in the pandemic years. This is a little technical – and boring, like most things related to banking – but please bear with me since it's a critical component of this segment of the consumer loans market.

Edtech loans work like this. The edtech company finds a lead (aka parents) and convinces the lead to buy a package/ product. The lead lacks the resources to pay the entire cost upfront. The edtech then goes to a fintech company, which arranges the funding and the terms of the loan. The fintech may, in fact, pass the loan on to a bank or a non-banking finance company (NBFC), which is actually providing the cash. The cost of the package is paid upfront to the edtech and the parent agrees to pay an EMI, or equated monthly instalment.

The fintech takes a fee (or two fees from the edtech and the NBFC), the NBFC has a high-interest borrower, and everything is fine so long as the parent keeps paying the EMI. These loans are unsecured, like most personal loans and unlike say, a loan for a car, there is nothing of much value to repossess beyond a used SD card and a low-end tablet.

Now, what happens if the borrower defaults? This is where the FLDG comes into the picture. FLDG, or the first loan default guarantee, is, as the name suggests, an arrangement between a fintech company and a lender – a bank or an NBFC. FLDG dictates that the fintech will compensate the lender to a certain extent in case a borrower defaults.

For example, let's suppose A is a borrower, B, the fintech company, and C is a lender, and C has lent A ₹100 through the good offices of B. A defaults, so now B has to compensate C for its loss. How much? That depends on how much B and C had agreed upon in the FLDG agreement. If there was a 20% FLDG, B would pay C ₹20 and so on and so forth.

Now, when the times are good and markets are rising, companies often get carried away. So, in boom times, a lot of companies signed FLDG agreements of 100% with the lenders. It gave them bragging rights, and showed lenders how confident they were about their business and the eventual customer. They got better terms. Lenders, of course, needed business and assumed their entire investment was secure – because they would get 100% of their money back even if the customer defaulted. So, they jumped in.

That's when things got interesting.

Byju's signed plenty of 100% FLDG contracts with third-party lenders. So, the customer buys the product, takes a loan and opts for EMIs. The lender pays Byju's in full. So far so good. Byju's takes this money, which could be anywhere between ₹35,000 to ₹1.5 lakh for a one-year or multi-year product, and books this entire amount as revenue for the year in which the sale was made. (This in itself is a poor accounting practice and we will explain later how problematic this eventually became for the company when the auditors finally woke up and red-flagged the practice.)

Now some days later, the customer says he wants to return

the product and seeks a refund. Byju's says it won't allow a refund for any of the numerous reasons it has written into the fine print. But the customer keeps chasing the company and refuses to pay the EMI. The bank or NBFC chases the customer for the EMI. It becomes a game of musical chairs.

At this point, the customer is faced with loan recovery agents and becomes the target of public shaming. Sometimes they end up paying the EMIs. But often, they stop paying. Ideally, in such cases, Byju's should pay the lender back whatever it is owed and close the case.

Once the lender realizes the customer can't be forced to pay the EMIs, the lender starts to haunt Byju's as well, and invokes the 100% FLDG agreement. Byju's then goes on radio silence for as long as it can, to delay paying up.

Around February 2023, while reporting for The Morning Context, I accessed loan statements and Byju's internal system screenshots for seven customers, who had cancelled their subscriptions, sought a refund and stopped paying EMIs. Instead of closing these subscriptions and returning the money to the lenders, I found out that the company was paying EMIs on behalf of the customer!

In the seven cases that I studied, the loan amounts ranged between ₹77,000 and ₹3 lakh. In five of these seven cases, the customers said that they had tried to cancel the contract before they stopped paying.

The financier was either Avanse Financial Services, or IIFL Finance, and all the loans were past due by over 180 days. In four of the cases, the customer didn't pay a single EMI. The internal system showed that the EMIs were being paid even though the customers were not paying them. In all these cases, EMIs had been credited through NEFT transactions after post-dated cheques had bounced.

The person who shared this data told me this: 'Byju's is paying the EMIs because they don't have the money to close the loans. There are probably more than 10,000–15,000 such live cases that are past due for 90 days or more. If you include the delay in the past few months for loans that finally closed, then we are looking at at least 40,000–50,000 cases.'

Earlier, the company used to process such loans within 30–40 days of default. But it got worse over time as cash flows deteriorated. Refunds were now processed as and when the company received money from new sales. At the time, this source estimated that such delayed payments could be to the tune of ₹500 crore. The company had achieved notoriety for creating a debt trap for parents. Now, it was creating a huge debt trap for itself, and it was also destroying the customers' credit ratings since every delay meant a black mark.

It got worse. Eventually, tired of the delays, and also in response to a policy change made by the RBI, fintechs stopped arranging loans to Byju's customers.

Remember the 100% FLDG agreement between Byju's and the lenders? In September 2022, RBI stated that a fintech company can only guarantee losses up to 5% of the loan size. It spooked the lenders and they eventually decided to cut their exposure in Byju's.

As a result, the company is now left with its own offerings – Byju's Assure, Byju's Advantage, and Byju's Direct – to provide customers with a line of credit. This puts immense pressure on its already strained cash flow.

This also effectively implies it is borrowing money to pay itself, or it is going through a complex transaction where it uses the cash from a customer who does pay upfront, to fund a loan for another customer. This also impacts the company's revenue going forward, of course.

While this step by lenders has slowed down the business – a lot of parents in smaller cities and villages could only afford Byju's products because there was a line of credit – there is no indication that the company's model of hard-selling to parents has changed one bit.

Salespeople are still pushed to the wall and they do whatever they need to make the sale happen. In June 2023, right after Deloitte Haskins & Sells resigned as the auditors and opened the Pandora's box of the company financials, NDTV caught up with some parents who told them how the company forced a sale and then denied them refunds. In one video clip, Sudarshana, a parent from Kolkata, recalls how she was asked to come and collect a certificate for a competition her son hadn't participated in and then coaxed into buying a product. She explains how the company promised a no-questions-asked, 15-day return policy, and then walked back on that promise.

4

The Edtech Boom

'Timing.'

This was Zishaan Hayath's succinct reply to my question 'Why edtech?'

'Could you please explain a little more?'

'Internet penetration was increasing [a universal phenomenon]; [the cost of] android phones had slipped to under $100, making computing personal and affordable [again, universal]; competitive exams had become or were becoming objective type; exams started going online instead of being paper-based. We [meaning the Indian edtech ecosystem] were at the intersection of these four trends.'

Hayath, who graduated from IIT Bombay in 2005, is an edtech pioneer. His platform Toppr.com launched in 2013, and it was the first serious player in the after-school online learning segment as we know it today. At the time, Raveendran was still taking classes across stadiums and Byju's Learning App was still in silent incubation. Vamsi Krishna had recently sold Lakshya Tutorials – an offline test-prep centre in Punjab – and moved to Bengaluru.

Toppr was a technology company in the field of education. It reimagined education delivery via technology. The others – Raveendran, Krishna of Vedantu, Gaurav Munjal and Roman Saini of Unacademy started as physical centres and extended their teaching models online. They used technology just as a tool. In that way, they were more like edupreneurs. Let me give you some examples to explain this better. Meru Cabs is a taxi services provider that was trying to build an app. Ola Cabs is essentially an app company that got into the cab business. The Future Group had retail businesses and tried to leverage technology to go digital, while Flipkart is a tech company that got into retail.

In the same vein, Hayath built education around technology and not the other way around. That is probably because unlike other edtech entrepreneurs, Hayath isn't a teacher. He is a products guy.

Hayath is a well-known face in the Mumbai start-up ecosystem. After finishing his engineering course, he dabbled a bit in the corporate world before co-founding Chaupaati Bazaar in 2008, one of the earliest phone commerce companies, where people could call and order a range of products, from magazines to home appliances. It became popular and, within three years, was acquired by the Future Group, then India's largest retailer. Hayath worked there till 2013 before starting Toppr.

Hayath liked to run and would use an app to measure his performance. He realized that the different parameters of the app helped him understand and improve the speed of his runs, his timing and efficiency. As it was, students and their parents were spending enormous amounts of time and money on after-school coaching classes. Given technology and some luck, he saw the opportunity to build a product that would replicate the after-school education model online.

'Hemanth [Goteti – his co-founder] and I wanted to create a technology company. We were thinking about ideas. We were looking at technology to solve a large problem,' Hayath says. 'Education fascinated us. You could do so much with technology in education. India has one of the largest student communities. So there was a huge opportunity for us to change how we learn by using technology while creating value for the company.'

Toppr started with its offerings from grade 5 onwards. It soon became popular for offering online classes, adaptive practice, endless question banks and mock papers on an intuitive app. One of the most interesting features of the Toppr app was the intuitive and adaptive nature of the product, where it would adapt to an individual's difficulty level and curate the material accordingly. It worked with the students, adapting to their pace and guiding them through tougher problems, one question at a time. It wasn't like a set template that gives you 10 easy questions and then kills your curiosity by throwing 5 difficult ones. It is not surprising that the app is still considered the best in class in the kindergarten to Grade 12 (K–12) segment by parents, teachers and edtech experts alike.

'This was the first time a young IITian was taking on the Kota and FIIT-JEE models inspired by Khan Academy-style videos,' says an edtech expert 'Alok' (name changed to protect identity) who has been tracking the industry for nearly two decades. 'Also, Zeeshan was a blue-eyed boy in the Powai IIT B angel ecosystem and that meant the entry of pro-investors. This jugalbandi [duet] started, in my opinion, what we know as the edtech wave today.'

Others followed soon.

Krishna launched Vedantu in 2014. Byju's launched The Learning App in 2015. Unacademy was launched as a YouTube channel the same year. The higher education and upskilling segment also saw a lot of action in 2015. Ronnie Screwvala, Mayank Kumar, Phalgun Kompalli and Ravijot Chugh came together to launch upGrad. Ashwin Damera and Chaitanya Kalipatnapu finally decided to take a leap of faith and launched Emeritus, the online platform for their venture Eruditus.

If you dig even deeper, you'll be able to trace the origin of education technology to the early 2000s. For India's education sector, 20 September 2004 was a red-letter day – that was when the Indian Space Research Organisation (ISRO) launched EDUSAT, a dedicated satellite for education, which revolutionized education.

One year later, TutorVista was born.

As the story goes, Krishnan Ganesh, a Delhi College of Engineering and IIM Calcutta alumnus, invested ₹50 lakh of his hard-earned money to develop a remote tutoring platform. The idea was simple. Students needed on-demand tutoring from qualified teachers. In India, this was a no-brainer; neighbourhood tutors and coaching centres had become part of the social fabric. But in the US, the UK or other developed parts of the world, it was still rare. And very expensive. About $40 per hour.

If someone could reduce those costs and still provide quality, on-demand tutoring, they could hit the jackpot. It made complete sense to outsource to India. Labour was cheap; Indians spoke English well; there was widespread market acceptance since the boom in information technology-enabled services had already generated the concept of being 'Bangalored' with back-end jobs being outsourced to India. Now with the technology available, one just needed to build a platform.

Ganesh played around with the idea for a bit before he went all in. He launched $100 per month unlimited one-on-one tuition sessions. He even trained teachers in teaching the US curriculum. The idea clicked. It also got investors interested.

Then in 2007, less than two years into the business, TutorVista acquired Edurite Technologies. The two companies were like chalk and cheese. TutorVista was new, slick, nimble and online. Edurite was old – it was incorporated in 2000 – and offline. It sold educational materials and management software to schools. After the acquisition, Edurite was renamed Manipal K–12 Education Pvt. Ltd. In 2009, the company entered the information and communications business for classrooms called DigiClass. Soon, offline became the focus area for TutorVista.

Then Pearson Education, the UK-based publishing and education company, came calling. It first bought a minority stake and eventually acquired TutorVista for about $150 million in 2011. What happened next depends on who you ask. The business wasn't doing well, debts increased, and there were problems with revenue recognition. But this much is undisputed: in 2017, Pearson sold the business to Byju's for a paltry $3 million. The rise and fall of TutorVista is a case study in itself and, on closer inspection, it is eerily similar to the trajectory Byju's is taking. Only the scale is different. Byju's is about billions, not paltry millions.

Business outcome notwithstanding, the fact is that TutorVista sowed the seeds of education technology in India.

Around the same time, there was another company that was scaling great heights. Educomp Solutions, started by IIM Ahmedabad alumnus Shantanu Prakash in 1994, went public in 2006. It started the smart-school movement in India by providing interactive content and compatible tools that would help Indian classrooms go digital. It was a novel attempt, and the new twist to the business model was ingenious. Educomp decided to take the business-to-business route and go directly to schools to tap the real potential of the schoolgoing population.

By January 2008, the Educomp scrip touched an all-time high of ₹1,130. For context, it was listed at ₹125. The company set up some 25 offices across the globe, expanded its customer base to close to 20,000 schools, and by 2012 its revenues touched ₹1,000 crore. Naturally, several other companies tried to take the same route.

But Educomp eventually fizzled out just as fast as it had grown. It took on more debt than it could handle and the company was forced to sell off its assets after its stock price crashed. It filed for bankruptcy in 2017. It is important to mention here that Educomp's problems went beyond debt.

'It was a case of exponential growth and the inability to manage it, leading to creative accounting and fudging of books,' the edtech expert tells me. 'Most of the current playbook of hard-selling and mis-selling, financial engineering with investors/debtors, EMIs, etc., were created then. On the back of Educomp's stock market listing, Everonn Systems went public and it met a similar fate. This "Ponzi-ness" of edtech started here.'

Educomp and TutorVista were the initial poster boys of Indian edtech. Pearson buying TutorVista demonstrated exit potential even though it turned out to be a bad acquisition for the buyer. It also showed investors were interested in novel education ideas that could scale. But both these businesses were in terrible shape around 2012–13. There was a lull in the market after the fall of Educomp and edtech was looking for its next successor. Toppr came along and claimed pole position.

——

It is important to understand the dynamics of the larger tech start-up ecosystem at the time. The period between 2013 and 2016 was crucial for the Indian start-up economy; it was the time when the start-up sector actually took off. To understand this, we need to dive deeper and navigate the dynamics of the global economy. So, allow me to make a short but necessary detour.

The US subprime crisis hit public consciousness when

investment bank Lehman Brothers went bankrupt in September 2008. It triggered a global economic meltdown. The US Federal Reserve then announced a slew of measures to keep the world economy from disintegrating. It created a range of emergency liquidity facilities to meet the needs of market participants.

One of the Fed's policy decisions was to lower interest rates to near-zero – that is negative in real terms after accounting for inflation. This created a lot of liquidity in financial markets, and some of that surplus liquidity eventually moved to high-yielding assets in emerging market economies, such as India. This was cheap money looking for big returns, and investors were, therefore, perfectly willing to accept very high risks.

It is important to remember here that despite the financial economy taking a hit, India escaped the full impact of the global economic meltdown. The Indian economy was not that deeply integrated with the global financial system and India's banks had practically no exposure to toxic US mortgages. The stock market index dropped by 65% in 2009 but the domestic economy continued to chug along. So India was also seen as something of a haven in troubled times.

The unprecedentedly gloomy global macroeconomic environment, contrasted with India's economic growth, made the country a hotbed for consumer start-ups. The watershed moment for Indian consumer internet companies came in 2013 when Flipkart raised $200 million from marquee investors like Tiger Global and Accel.

In 2015, venture capitalists doubled the amount they had pumped into Indian start-ups to nearly $5.5 billion, as companies such as Ola Cabs, Paytm, Flipkart and Grofers raised hundreds of millions of dollars. VCs were betting heavily on all the consumer segments from food tech to delivery to travel. A lot of money flowed into education technology as well. According to a 2018 Nasscom report on the edtech landscape, 2015 saw the emergence of over 1,000 start-ups in edtech, raising more than $125 million in funding. Per capita disposable income was rising, as was awareness about digital edtech.

At this point, it seemed that the only obstacle that prevented the democratization of quality education was mobile telephony and internet penetration. Internet penetration in India stood at around 30% in 2015, according to the periodical reports released by Telecom Regulatory Authority of India (TRAI). It was a lot better than 7.5% in 2010, but it also meant that over 1 billion people still had no access to the internet. That changed the next year.

In a 2012 piece for *Forbes*, Joshua Kim mentioned that a large mobile phone user base will be one big reason for the adoption of education technology in the future. Kim was then the director of learning and technology for the Master of Health Care Delivery Science programme at Dartmouth College. He suggested in the piece that India was set to leapfrog campus-based higher education and jump right to online learning. He predicted that the first trend – the adoption of mobile phones – would catalyse the second change, the penetration of online learning.

Although this was said in the context of higher education, this prophecy proved to be true across all segments in edtech when Reliance Jio launched in late 2016.

To say that Jio revolutionized internet telephony would be an understatement. It introduced broadband services at way cheaper prices, forcing a price war, and also taking internet to every corner of the country. For a majority of Indians, their first internet experience was on their smartphones on Jio's network. In a 2019 report, the Telecom Regulatory Authority of India said that the cost of mobile data had fallen by about 95% (to ₹11.78 per GB) in the three short years since the launch of Jio.

Cheaper data had a ripple effect on the tech start-up ecosystem. Given so many people were consuming data over smartphones, these start-ups had a large addressable market. Thanks to the price war started by Jio, the cost of reaching out to this addressable market was now much lower.

The financial technology sector – and India has one of the most robust fintech ecosystems with hundreds of service providers ranging from Paytm to Razorpay to Google Pay – is built on the back of cheap data. The entire digital public infrastructure, including concepts like the UPI and Aadhaar authentication, is built on cheap mobile broadband data. This is, in fact, one of the many reasons why venture capital firms remain bullish about India.

As the pandemic struck and things became remote and contactless, online transactions – from remote learning to digital payments to deliveries and e-commerce – reached escape velocity. Internet penetration, which had been around 30% in 2015, reached the 57% mark in 2023. The latest data indicates that between them, Jio (448 million internet users), Airtel (248 million) and Vodafone Idea (124 million Internet users) serviced over 800 million users on mobile broadband as of June 2023 – that's roughly 57% penetration. Another 30 million Indians use fixed broadband via fibre (there's overlap, of course, in that most fixed line broadband users also use mobile broadband).

———

The growth of mobile broadband changed the face of Indian edtech. Suddenly, there was a queue of investors, all making a beeline for the edtech pie. Between 2016 and 2019, edtech companies raised more than $1.5 billion in venture capital, according to data from Venture Intelligence.

But money was just one factor – focus was another. By 2019, a large number of experimental edtech start-ups were raising money and differentiating themselves by focusing on niches such as coding, activity and experiment-based learning, upskilling, what-have-you.

The income-sharing agreement model, where you pay the company after you get a job placement, arrived in India during this period. Massive open online courses became more popular as more people got access to the internet. This too was a result of the combination of several factors. It was a function of excess liquidity in the market and investors betting on the India story, and parents also realizing there is more to edtech than just academic learning.

Byju's received more than $900 million of all the edtech funding that came to India during this period. A $25 million investment from Sequoia Capital India just before The Learning App was launched in 2015 also gave the company some serious validation since Sequoia is an A-list VC. It enabled an already aggressive company to go into overdrive.

Within nine months, Byju's raised another round from Sequoia and Sofina. The $75 million fundraise was the largest capital infusion in an Indian edtech company at the time. The company used the funds to add more subjects and grades, grow its team, and expand to new geographies. In a matter of months, the company raised more money, another $50 million, this time from the Chan Zuckerberg Initiative. Again, this investment meant more than money; it was validation from a tech legend.

Mark Zuckerberg's Facebook post announcing this investment got a million or so likes. Not only did it yield good press coverage, but it also translated into more downloads of The Learning App. By September 2016, Byju's had more than 7 million downloads and over 300,000 paying subscribers. The company had now employed around 1,000 people across verticals.

In 2017, the Harvard Business School did a case study on how Byju's was impacting learning. Money brought growth and growth, money, in what seemed like a virtuous circle – Byju's was on a high. By the end of 2018, the company had become India's first edtech unicorn – a start-up with a valuation north of $1 billion.

So, Toppr started the current edtech movement, but Byju's took the baton and ran away with it.

The money was supposed to help start-ups create digital platforms to cut the clutter of messy physical education infrastructure, and give everyone (with a smartphone) access to quality education. Edtech was supposed to democratize education. This idea of democratization is pivotal to the idea of edtech.

Hayath explained this in an interview with The Morning Context. In offline coaching centres or tuitions, he told me, parents have no idea about the teacher. They don't know whether they had any impact on students in the last five years. 'We have more data on our food delivery guys than we have on our tuition teachers, or coaching classes,' he told me.

> Coaching classes are discriminatory. They are expensive. So people from the financially weaker sections of society don't have access to them. There are geographical limits to coaching centres. Then they are bubble-sorted: the best students go to the top sections and the best teachers go to the top sections to teach the best students. And the best-performing students get their fees refunded. So I am thinking from the perspective of a parent of an average student: what is happening here? My child is paying the full fees to get the worst teacher and to subsidize the fee of the best student. I did not sign up for this. If you think in that context, technology has made it an equal opportunity business. Whether you are a student from Banjara Hills, or Malabar Hills, or you live in a middle-income neighbourhood in Jabalpur, you have equal access to content.

Another set of numbers, which I received from Damera, the co-founder of Eruditus, may illustrate this point better. The gross enrolment ratio in India is about 27% for colleges. That means out of 100 kids who finish school, only 27 go to college. In absolute terms, that number is close to about 40 million students. The gross enrolment ratio in the US is about 80%, 60–65% in the UK and 40% in China.

If India is to raise the ratio to 40% in 10 years, we will need about 20 million new university seats at the minimum. Can you do that by opening offline institutions? The answer is no. Now, while this might have been said in the context of higher education, it is equally true for all segments.

While online learning was taking off, the age-old and time-tested physical coaching businesses were still struggling to find investor interest. Some – Aakash Educational Services and FIITJEE, for example – even experimented with the online format. But these experiments didn't yield much.

Coaching centres are a capital-intensive business. Leasing space, building infrastructure and setting up classrooms, among other things, cost a fortune. These are one-time costs. Add overheads like recurring salaries and utility bills and you realize that the cost of running a centre is pretty high. And, capacity is limited since there are only a fixed number of students one can accommodate in a given classroom. The margins in the offline model, therefore, are quite low. It takes months, sometimes years, to make a coaching centre profitable.

Coaching centres are also difficult to scale. Lower margins apart, space is finite. There is a limited number of physical classrooms that can be built. Then, there is competition and other logistical issues. For example, how many centres can a popular teacher visit?

Coaching centres are also highly fragmented. When a centre becomes successful and reaches scale, further fragmentation happens as teachers branch out, or competition increases. You have to keep watching your back all the time. Kota is an example of how hyper-competitive this business can get.

Also, few centres except the marquee ones make serious money. Then there is also the threat of poaching of teachers by other institutes. As a result, in the last 60–70 years, no clear pan-India leader has emerged in the offline coaching centre business.

'If you look at coaching centre chains, only their main centres are profitable. The rest don't make money,' one edtech insider who has been involved in both offline and online businesses tells me. 'That's why even the most successful ones like Aakash, Allen, etc., are limited to certain geographies. There are so many fires to fight constantly that it is impossible to expand geographically.'

'If you talk to Aakash and Allen, you will see that their biggest problem is expansion and capex,' says another industry expert. 'Scale in the offline business is a function of many things: a large base of trained teachers, infrastructure and logistics, systems and technology, ground coverage and its unit economics, consistent delivery every day in every classroom, and an inspiring culture to keep teaching and non-teaching staff as well as students happy. It is a long process and a very expensive one.'

Venture investors want growth, returns, positive

momentum even when the market is down and, finally, a handsome exit option. Every dollar of VC funding comes with riders. VCs also work on 7–10-year timelines, which – and on this, every offline coaching centre operator agrees – is not enough time to create a sustainable and profitable coaching centre business.

It won't be wrong to say that the trajectories of VC/PE investors, and their expected timelines of growth and returns move in a different direction from that of the offline coaching centre business. The only noticeable exception has been Aakash Education Services. In 2018, Akash received the go-ahead from the Securities and Exchange Board of India for a public offering but decided against it. One year later, in October 2019, the offline test prep company received ₹1,350 crore from PE firm Blackstone, which picked up a 37.5% stake in the company. The deal valued Aakash at $500 million.

5

The Hand of God

Tuesday, 12 January 2021.

I had just put my 18-month-old to bed and settled down with a warm drink and my laptop. It was a cold evening in Delhi but I was looking forward to a promising Wednesday meeting. I was supposed to catch up with Aakash Chaudhry, who was then the managing director of Aakash Educational Services Ltd.

I had to prepare for this interview. I was keen to meet him because a few weeks before – we (meaning The Morning Context) had identified the company as Indian edtech's dark horse in 2021. This was after everyone, including us, had written epitaphs for the offline coaching centres business. It was going to be one exciting meeting.

In came a Slack notification. Then a text message. Then more beeps. And then, chaos.

Bloomberg had just reported that Byju's had acquired Aakash for around $1 billion in a cash and stock deal. This sent newsrooms into a frenzy. My meeting with Aakash was postponed indefinitely.

Not only was this one of the biggest edtech acquisitions in the world, but it was also a defining moment in India's edtech history. Even by Raveendran's standards, it was an audacious move.

Here was a five-year-old company, with a big war chest of VC dollars and high on the boost the pandemic had given to online activity. It was taking over a 33-year-old giant in the coaching industry.

At the time, Byju's had three things going for it: a robust sales engine; the charismatic founder who could raise money from anywhere at the drop of a hat, which kept boosting the valuation of the company; and third, and not to be underestimated, its multimillion-dollar marketing expenditure that already made it into a household name. Other things, like the efficacy of its product, the learning outcomes, levels of customer satisfaction, etc., were not even question marks; they weren't even spoken about when the company was the topic of discussion.

In terms of business models, the two businesses were wildly different. Aakash was a well-established brand with a proven track record. It was built on word of mouth, one brick at a time. It had, and still has, enviable brand recall, a clean balance sheet, and, most importantly, it was making a profit, which is a distant dream for most unicorns.

Byju's was online, Aakash offline. Byju's was all about scaling, Aakash about slow, sustainable growth. Byju's spoke about learning; Aakash, about outcomes. As said above, the two businesses were like night and day.

To take a billion-dollar bet on a business so different was considered just crazy, according to everyone. Raveendran told me during one of our calls that just about everyone he had spoken to had told him he had overvalued Aakash and was paying around 20% premium over fair valuation for the deal.

Another edtech expert, who had done some due diligence for a client, told me that Byju's was paying at least 30% more than their estimation of Aakash's value at the time. If you remember, Blackstone Group's investment in the offline coaching company, in October 2019, valued it at just $500 million so these guesstimates of overvaluation are credible and maybe conservative.

Whatever the merits of the acquisition and how it unfolded, this one deal ushered in a new dawn in India's edtech industry. It made it apparent that the new-age, nimbler online competitors were taking over from the old guard, the somewhat jaded, offline education businesses. It also showed that investors had the appetite to take bold bets. It marked the beginning of a new world order. It was the best illustration of how Covid-19 with its buzzwords of WFH (work from home) and distance learning had changed the shape of the industry.

This was hardly the first time that Byju's was going the mergers and acquisitions route. Ever since the VC funding had started flowing, the company had been on the lookout for interesting 'buys'.

This is a perfectly legitimate way for a business to 'inorganically' acquire the competencies it needs. In some of the mergers and acquisitions cases, the synergies were obvious. In others, it may have been arguable. But Aakash was so wildly different from Byju's and the sums involved were so large, it raised eyebrows across the VC ecosystem.

Acquisitions by Byju's (2011–2023*)

Target Company	Sub-Sector	Amount ($Mn)	Deal Type	Date
Vidyartha	Online Services – Career Guidance	1	Domestic	Jan 2017
Edurite Technologies*	Online Services – Education	1	Domestic	Jul 2017
TutorVista**	Online Services – Remote Tutoring	1	Domestic	Jul 2017
Math Adventures	Equipment – Educational Kits	2	Domestic	Jul 2018
Osmo	Equipment – Tablet	120	Outbound	Jan 2019
WhiteHat Jr	Coding for Kids	300	Domestic	Aug 2020
LabInApp	K–12 – Science Lab Work	N.A.	Domestic	Sep 2020
Aakash Educational Services	Test Preparation	1,000	Domestic	Jan 2021
Scholr	On-demand Homework Help	NA	Domestic	Feb 2021
HashLearn	Remote Tutoring	N.A.	Domestic	May 2021
Epic	Reading	500	Outbound	Jul 2021
Great Learning	Upskilling	600	Domestic	Jul 2021
Toppr	Test Preparation	150	Domestic	Jul 2021
Whodat	Augmented Reality	N.A.	Domestic	Aug 2021

Target Company	Sub-Sector	Amount ($Mn)	Deal Type	Date
Gradeup	Test Preparation	N.A.	Domestic	Sep 2021
Tynker	Coding for Kids	200	Outbound	Sep 2021
CultureAlley	Cloud-based Language Learning Platform	25	Domestic	Nov 2021*
GeoGebra	Online Services – Education	100	Outbound	Dec 2021

*Around November 2021; **Indicates asset sale
Data as of 31 July 2023.
Source: Venture Intelligence

The pandemic-induced lockdown did for edtech what demonetization did for digital payments.

Between 2015 and 2019, the edtech sector was growing but at a relatively slower rate. There was still resistance in the minds of Indian parents regarding online education. The coronavirus outbreak broke through this mental barrier as schools were forced to go online.

Lockdowns opened up a world of new possibilities for edtech companies, which rushed in to fill the learning gap as schools were forced shut and millions of students were confined to their homes. According to a UNESCO report, the pandemic affected over 1.5 billion students globally. It also made governments and institutions around the globe look at online learning in a different light. In India, Amit Khare, secretary in India's Ministry of Human Resource Development, which handles education, wrote a letter on 20 March 2020 to chief secretaries across states and Union Territories, asking them to optimize e-learning 'during the coming days'.

Like their peers around the world, India's leading online learning companies started offering students free access to their platform and content. Byju's, with over 42 million users and a valuation north of $8 billion at the time, announced on 11 March that it was making its learning programmes for students in grades 1 through 12 free till April end. Soon after, its Mumbai-based rival Toppr made access to its live and video classes free till 31 March. Test prep start-up Unacademy announced 20,000 free live classes for candidates preparing for various entrance exams. Upgrad, which offers online upskilling programmes for professionals, made access to its upGrad Live platform free for all colleges and universities. Edtech saw the lockdowns as a golden opportunity.

'This is an opportunity for us to generate trials,' Hayath told me at the time. 'It is a great time for parents to experience online learning themselves and for schools to decide how it works for them.'

Convincing parents to take a trial used to be an arduous task. Remember the counselling calls? In normal times, trials on such a massive scale would have been impossible. No government or education board would have agreed to an experiment of switching to online learning. But this was an extraordinary situation. Even perpetually busy parents had plenty of time. As they spent more time indoors, their engagement with their children increased. Betting on free access and increased parental engagement, edtech companies started aiming to sign up as many users as they could, in the hope that free users would eventually convert to become paid subscribers when the tide turned.

This is what people in marketing call the top of the funnel. Companies spend hundreds of hours and hundreds of millions of dollars to create this top of the funnel for their businesses. The pandemic gave edtech companies an unbelievable top of the funnel on a scale they could have never imagined and all without spending a dime on marketing.

By most estimates, demand soared. Byju's reported a 60% increase in the number of students using its products once it made its app free.

As the lockdown went from days to weeks to months, the government also jumped into action. It introduced the National Education Policy, 2020 on 29 July, the first such policy in 34 years, with an aim to digitize the country's education system. The focus was on online learning. In the aftermath of the pandemic, when everything from baby showers to wakes moved online, it was inevitable.

Section 23 of the policy is dedicated to the use of technology and its integration. It talks about the adoption of emerging and disruptive technologies such as AI and robotics, the creation of a National Educational Technology Forum to advise central and state governments on technology-based interventions, build intellectual and institutional capacities in educational technology and articulate new directions for research and innovation.

The policy also envisions the creation of an open, transformed, and evolvable e-learning digital infrastructure to increase the reach of education. It suggests the use of tech tools in better preparation of teachers as well as improving the teaching, learning and evaluation process. It even recommended the initiation of coding for students as early as grade 6. This is the first time in the history of the country that so much emphasis has been given to technology and its use in education.

In the meantime, online learning was galloping ahead at breakneck speed. According to an April 2021 Ernst & Young report on online learning platforms in India, the top 100 education websites recorded around 150% growth in page views in the six months between March and October 2020. The consistency in the number of page views over months was, as the report suggests, a sign of stickiness to the model.

This was an extraordinary time. These numbers were unprecedented. The industry was exploding. It was so sudden that no one could afford to take a moment to introspect before acting. Edtech companies, which had marketed their wares through leveraging FOMO, now experienced FOMO themselves as they feared being left behind and relegated to oblivion.

It also created FOMO among investors who didn't want to miss the edtech bandwagon. Investors saw returns in the stickiness of the model and rushed in. Money brought in more money and this created a feedback loop. First, it boosted the valuation of companies massively and also provided them with the financial fuel they needed to motor on at top speed. The higher valuations also made it easier for them to raise even more cash.

The frenetic nature of the action is reflected in the deal activity between March 2020 and the first half of 2022. That was the high tide where investments into edtech was concerned. In 2023, interest has faded as the data indicates.

VC Investments in Edtech Start-ups in India (2015–2023*)

Period	No. of Deals	Amount ($Mn)
2015	38	87
2016	41	205
2017	38	151
2018	51	690
2019	57	429
2020	77	2,220
2021	112	4,165
2022	75	2,103
2023*	23	172

* Data as of 25 September 2023
Source: Venture Intelligence

Private equity and venture capital investments into edtech just exploded. According to another Ernst & Young report, PE/VC investment in edtech between 2020 and 2022 accounted for more than 70% of the total investment in the sector since 2010. According to data from Venture

Intelligence, the sector received nearly $7 billion in VC investments between April 2020 and June 2022. With cheques worth $3.3 billion to its name, Byju's accounted for more than half of this investment, while Eruditus received $763 million and Unacademy $730 million.

In 2021, the Chinese government took a landmark decision that not only changed the future of edtech companies in that country but also had a massive impact on their counterparts in India. On Saturday, 24 July 2021, the world's second-largest economy unveiled sweeping education policy changes. The PRC banned edtech start-ups that taught the school curriculum through the compulsory years of education from making profits, or going public, or raising capital in other ways. Companies that taught school subjects could no longer accept overseas funding. Listed firms were banned from raising capital from the stock markets to invest in companies that taught school subjects. Acquisitions went off limits as did weekend tutoring.

It is important to note that the education market in China and India have many similarities.

China and India have the world's first and second largest education system, respectively, and the two countries are home to nearly half the world's primary-school-age children, according to a 2003 paper by Nirmala Rao, Kai-Ming Cheng and Kirti Narain. The two countries started building their education system in similar conditions in the 1940s. The national leaders of both countries perceived education as an integral part of development. Both nations faced similar challenges in building a robust education system, while going through a rapid industrial and social transformation.

While China has forged far ahead in many ways, what hasn't changed is the importance given to education in both societies. Children attending school and college is top priority for parents in both countries. As in India, education is seen as the great equalizer in China as well. Chinese parents also send their children to after-school tuitions and China's education sector, like India's, is fiercely competitive.

China's education sector is focused on the gaokao, or the college entrance exam, which fuels the private on-demand tutoring industry. In cities like Beijing, Shanghai, Guangzhou and Shenzhen, 70% of the students in kindergarten through grade 12 receive after-school tutoring. The tutoring boom has led to a heavy workload on students and a significant financial burden on parents. Especially during the lockdown, it triggered social inequality among China's urban and rural populations. Calling out the industry's 'disorderly development', President Xi Jinping called it a 'social problem'.

In announcing the rules, China's education ministry said: 'In recent years, a large amount of capital has poured into educational training . . . adverts are everywhere, bombarding the whole of society . . . It has destroyed the normal environment for education.'

So the government decided to nuke the equalizer.

In one decisive move, the Chinese government killed the edtech industry that was worth $100 billion. Shares of listed education companies and investors in Chinese edtech start-ups got hammered.

China, prior to the policy change, was home to 8 out of the world's 28 edtech unicorns, according to global impact intelligence platform Holon IQ. The PRC's edtech industry attracted $10 billion in 2020, accounting for nearly two-thirds of VC investments in education globally, from the likes of Alibaba, Tiger Global, Tencent, SoftBank, Sequoia Capital and GGV Capital.

The move, part of a larger crackdown on private tech businesses in the country that started with cutting Alibaba and Jack Ma to size, wiped out more than $1 trillion from the market value of big tech companies in China. Edtech entrepreneurs say it also resulted in pushing a lot of capital to India. This was a specific instance where the 'China-plus-one' investment strategy of global institutional investors and VC/PE was turbocharged by Chinese government intervention.

Apart from the China angle, there was also FOMO on two levels. First, big VC firms that had given edtech companies a pass in their early stages. With the lockdown and exponential growth in traffic and valuations of edtech companies, this was their moment of redemption. Second, for several marquee VC funds, which had missed out on the India story earlier, this was their chance to make amends.

'Remember, Sequoia Capital India (now Peak XV Partners) missed out on Flipkart and even Ola Cabs. There was no chance it would, or could, miss sectors like edtech, quick commerce, food delivery, etc.,' an edtech executive told me. 'There is always pressure when you miss out on such opportunities and when you see the next one coming, you go all out. And, as they used to say, where Sequoia goes, everyone follows.'

This mad rush created five new edtech unicorns in India. This was unthinkable even five years ago. On the back of the fresh investments, Byju's valuation grew nearly threefold from $8 billion in March 2020 to $22 billion in March 2022.

High valuation is appealing, trending and sexy. It makes for great headlines. But often they are just that: headlines. Indicative, at best. Vanity, at worst. Most times, valuations don't mean much, because valuations are not real unless they are in listed companies where the shares can be traded in large volumes. In PE and VC investments, the valuation is a number that two people agree upon. Sometimes, that agreement is casually doodled on a napkin in a bar between the fourth and fifth round of drinks.

Founders are biased towards their product and will always want a higher valuation for their company. All they need is one investor to believe their story. So, the smart operators build a narrative, show a potential to disrupt and to scale. Given a country of 1.4 billion and the wide world beyond, it's easy to create hype about future growth prospects.

In a bull market, when there is liquidity around, excel sheets with fancy numbers will fly. Someone will take a bite and with some luck, a whole cycle of FOMO will begin. With each round of fundraising, the valuation will soar, even if the fundamentals of the business don't change much.

The lockdown was one such boom period. Just as in the subprime crisis, central banks responded to the trauma of Covid-19 by cutting interest rates and releasing a flood of liquidity. Given that half the world's industries were in lockdown, that cash was seeking billets and edtech was an obvious possibility as everybody went online.

The billions of dollars of investment coming to India had one unintended but inevitable consequence: inflated valuations. And it wasn't just edtech, this occurred across the tech start-up ecosystem. It would become a problem eventually, but that came later.

———

Given the enthusiasm of investors with deep pockets, the pursuit of growth became the one-point agenda for edtech companies. It didn't matter where the growth came from, and sustainability was not even a consideration. Companies expanded to smaller cities and launched courses for multiple state boards. Vedantu, for example, launched micro-courses. Everyone tried their hand at multilanguage offerings. Toppr partnered with the Ryan Group to roll out its integrated platform School OS.

Where these companies could not expand, they acquired. They also started diversifying into new product categories. Acquisitions gave the edtech biggies a foothold in doubt-solving, test prep, higher education, offline education and gamification in India and abroad.

Vedantu, for example, acquired doubt-solving platform Instasolv. Byju's was pursuing Doubtnut, though talks fizzled out. Unacademy used mergers and acquisitions to get into upskilling and even into placements. Everyone wanted a piece of the coding pie. Unacademy acquired CodeChef in June 2020. Next month, Toppr launched Toppr Codr to teach K–12 students coding.

Byju's went a step further and acquired WhiteHat Jr for a record $300 million in August. It doubled down its bet on coding with the acquisition of Tynker, a California-based coding platform for K–12 students, in September 2021. Tynker, founded by Krishna Vedati, Srinivas Mandyam and Kelvin Chong in Mountain View, California, in 2012, teaches children aged between 5 and 18 how to code.

The Tynker deal was the Indian company's third acquisition in the US and came close on the heels of the acquisition of the reading platform Epic. It was a strong indication of Byju's growing ambitions in the North American market. Raveendran had been looking for a slice of the US market since 2016, but had little luck before the pandemic. He bought Tangible Play Inc., the parent company of Osmo, a digital learning and gaming platform for children, in 2019. But this hadn't contributed much to the Indian company's balance sheet. Still, Raveendran wasn't giving up on the US market.

He knew or suspected growth in the home market would taper soon and admitted as much in a TV interview. Hence, the company had to look overseas to keep expanding at a rapid rate. The question was where. Since China was out of the question after the crackdown, the US market had become even more critical. It was Karan Bajaj's ability to tap the US market through his coding start-up WhiteHat Jr that made it a lucrative target.

In general, the US is the holy grail for tech start-ups, their ultimate test. It is a market with a unique understanding of tech products and, therefore, you have scores of start-ups jostling for the American customer's attention. Survive that, and the world becomes your oyster. It is too appealing a prospect for any tech company to ignore. But the flip side of this is that the US market is also ruthless. Only 1 in 10 start-ups survive in the long run. The global ambitions of many entrepreneurs have been sacrificed at the altar of their US ambitions.

Zomato, for example, entered the US market in 2015, tried different things and, eventually, shut down the US business just before it went public in 2021. Or take OYO, the budget hotel chain that entered the US in 2019. It took barely a year for hotel owners to find out that OYO's business is all bait and switch.

But Raveendran was doubling down. He told *Business Today*'s Udayan Mukherjee that the company would move fast and invest $1 billion in the next three years in the US, which, in turn, would generate $1 billion in revenue.

Raveendran believed that Byju's new portfolio of US companies was under-monetized and could be scaled at a faster pace. So, he raised $1.2 billion via a term loan B arrangement in the US in November 2021 to fund and manage inorganic growth. By now, Byju's had become a sort of private equity fund, taking bets in edtech that were too hot for even hardened VCs.

Between March 2020 and June 2022, Byju's acquired 11 companies, some of which have made their own acquisitions since. Unacademy, in the same period, acquired 10 companies. At one point, the two companies were in talks with each other for a merger/acquisition. The competition to become the world's largest edtech conglomerate was real. With Beijing delivering a death sentence to China's edtech industry, it was looking quite possible.

After two years of relentless growth, the Byju's juggernaut was on a roll. The company was raising money and acquiring companies at an alarming frequency. Thanks to its acquisitions, Byju's expanded into new markets like the US and the Middle East. It was everywhere. On billboards, on TV, online. On the jerseys of India's cricket teams, and visible at the football World Cup in Qatar. The company proudly paraded Lionel Messi and Shah Rukh Khan as its brand ambassadors.

By March 2022, the company had more than 58,000 employees, according to data from the EPFO sourced from corporate data provider Private Circle. It was growing in all directions. Raveendran had been talking about crossing ₹10,000 crore in revenue for the 12-month period to 31 March 2021. He was also planning to take the company public to unlock its potential. He had wanted exponential growth for the company in 2017. By 2022, riding on the back of a pandemic and a lockdown, he got exactly that.

The pandemic led to millions of deaths and caused untold misery to hundreds of millions who suffered unemployment and health crises. But for the Indian edtech industry, it was like the hand of God, a divine intervention that gave them an open goal. It drove students willy-nilly into online distance-learning and whatever misgivings parents may have had about virtual schooling, they were left with no choice.

As such, the pandemic created the opportunity for exponential growth. But there is a problem with exponential growth. It puts a massive strain on the system to keep growing and ultimately becomes unsustainable. The Byju's juggernaut was heading in that direction by the time Covid-19 was easing off.

6

The Tyranny of Targets

Planning to screw one more day?
Before breaking for lunch, ensure everyone is at 4 bookings
No one will leave for lunch without meeting me
After 7 pm, if I see anyone on break, you will be suspended
from next day, It's our session time and you have no sense of
responsibility
No need to report to office from tomorrow
Say no to follow up [emphasis theirs]
Only on spot closing
Everyone get into sessions and close deals on spot
No one would be giving to time to any cx [sic]
*Remember **No Follow Ups*** [emphasis theirs]
Let's not leave any cx available at hand without closing.
No one should come out of the session without closing.
Need you all to be super aggressive.
People giving waste attitudes, trust I will make you suffer like
hell under me if you are not aligned with your seniors.

These are snippets from texts sent out by managers to

salespeople at Byju's offices in Bengaluru. I've seen many more salty statements that really can't be published due to the casual obscenity on display. Incidentally, the gender ratio in the Byju's salesforce was around 80:20 in favour of males, until it moved to a telemarketing 'inside sales' model, when it changed to around 60:40 M:F.

Swearing is common if not endemic. It's like a teledrama with yelling in lieu of background music. Managers openly threaten to make a salesperson – business development associate/executive (BDA/BDE) in corporate speak – 'suffer' and face consequences, including asking the human resources department to put them on performance watch, if they don't make their targets or align with seniors.

'It emanates from the incessant pressure of targets,' says Pratik Makhija. 'If you meet your initial target, a new target is given. It is a never-ending race to the top that no one can see. It is complete chaos.'

When I interviewed him for a story on the work culture of Byju's for The Morning Context in August 2022, Makhija, then 27, was a senior business development associate at Byju's and spoke on condition of anonymity. He has since left the company.

This was actually his second innings at Byju's. In his first stint, Makhija had worked with the company as a senior business development associate between July 2019 and January 2021. He tells me that it was the insane work culture that had made him leave.

But Makhija returned in July 2022. He needed money and the company was offering a good salary. Things, however, had somehow become worse, he says. It made him speak up for himself and others. Result? He was suspended for weeks. He eventually left again in October 2022.

Makhija talked about a toxic work culture of systemic abuse – physical, verbal and psychological. He described working conditions that left 20-something fresh graduates with lifestyle diseases, and a job that forced people to cross ethical boundaries. He also talked about a leadership that, despite knowing everything, chose to be silent spectators on the sidelines.

Makhija's descriptions are in sync with more than a hundred salespeople I have spoken with in nearly four years of reporting on the company. Every one of them described the same toxic culture and all of them requested anonymity for fear of a backlash.

In August 2022, when I wrote about the work culture, Byju's did not respond to questions sent over email. But in multiple interactions before and after, Raveendran and Mohit have flatly denied the existence of such an abusive culture.

When I asked Mohit in 2020 why many salespersons complained about long working hours and stiff targets, this is what he had to say: 'We have the best people. In fact, our competitors hire salespeople from us. We have the best processes and a strong HR team. So, this shouldn't happen, but I take your point. As far as sales are concerned, it was difficult when we launched in 2015. People didn't know us. I used to make about a hundred calls a day. Those were difficult times. Today, we have a brand. People trust us and take pride in what they buy.'

The issue has since been highlighted by many publications, and in each of these reports the company's spokesperson has maintained that Byju's has the best HR practices and takes utmost care of its employees.

The claims are belied, however, by an enormous amount of contradictory evidence that back up the assertions made by the many employees I have spoken with over a period of nearly four years.

I have seen messages on WhatsApp, heard audio recordings of calls and meetings, and read internal emails – marked to everyone, including Raveendran, Mohit, Gokulnath and the HR team – which substantiate multiple claims of toxic work culture made by employees. These are in complete contrast with the claims made by the management, who have, over the years, ignored these messages and encouraged this abusive atmosphere rather than attempting to put a stop to it.

Byju's relentless pursuit of growth put its systems – including the enviable sales engine that brought the exponential growth – under tremendous strain. The gap between the ideas leaving the corner office and the reality on the sales floor is widening even now, as the vision of the future gets even more clouded with each passing week.

———

The offices in Bengaluru are the worst, say salespeople. Work is still manageable, if not enjoyable, at other locations. At least, work timings are fixed at centres outside Bengaluru. An employee can log out of the office, switch off completely, pick up the threads of their personal life, and log in to fight the good fight again the next day.

In Bengaluru, they can't. To start with, the punch-in time is officially around 10 a.m., but managers demand that salespeople report by 9 a.m., come hell or high water. There's a meeting every morning. I have heard recordings of several meetings when seniors gather salespersons in a circle and ask about their timings and the number of sales.

The senior sounds like a feudal king or zamindar holding court. These calls would be funny if they weren't tragic. Here's the transcript of a small section of one call between a senior manager and salespersons, which I have edited for clarity and length. Read it for yourself and draw your own conclusions.

Senior manager: The timing is not 10 a.m. The timing is 9 a.m. What time did you all come to work today? How many of you were here at 9 a.m.?

Salesperson 1: Sir, I.

SM: You were? Okay. [Talks to the next person] You?

SP 2: 8.30 a.m.

SM: Very good. [Asks the third person] You?

SP 3: Sir, 9.15 a.m.

SM: Come at 9 a.m. No delays, not even 15 minutes. Pandey, 10 a.m. or 11 a.m., when did you come?

Pandey: Sir, 9.45.

SM: Why 9.45? Weren't you told to report at 9 a.m.?

Pandey: Sir, actually I had an issue.

SM: What issue? Whatever the issue. Did the manager not tell you to come at 9 a.m.? Is he a ch****ya to tell you something and you won't listen to him [*sic*]? Are you above the manager?

Pandey: Sir, my bike's keys—

SM [stopping him mid-sentence]: I was also a BDA. Bike's keys, flat tyre, traffic, accidents, I have seen it all. Already done. That's why I am sitting here. So don't try to bullshit me. If your manager is telling you something, it is coming from me. Not obeying your manager is equal to not obeying me. The time for tomorrow is 9 a.m. I will specifically check your time tomorrow. So, if the bike's key is an issue, get another one made. Get five sets of spare keys. Ensure that this is taken care of.

[Moves on to the next salesperson] What time did you come in today?

SP 4: Sir, 9.25 a.m.

SM: You are saying 9.25 like it is 8.30 a.m. What is the time you should reach the office on Saturdays and Sundays?

SP 4: Sir [referring to his manager] told me to come at 9.30. I reported at 9.25.

[SM calls the manager.]

SM: What time did you ask them to report?

Manager: Sir, 9.30.

SM: Why 9.30? I told you 9 a.m.

Manager: Sir, everyone's demos—

SM [interrupting him]: I told you to call everyone at 9. Ensure everyone is at work tomorrow at 9 a.m. And you be here at 8.30. Got it? You come in at 8.30 and message me. If you are not here, why will they be there?

It is an hour-long voice clip that just keeps getting worse. I will spare you the details but you can guess how this would carry on. Officially, their day gets over at 7 p.m. but, in reality, their log-out time is completely at the mercy of managers.

'If we try to leave at even 10 p.m., managers would say: "Where are you going? The work has just started,"' Makhija says. 'If we say we have been at work since morning, they would say, "Show us how many calls you have logged. How many bookings have you confirmed?" As a result, we are in the office till 11 p.m. on most days.'

'We return home past midnight. Often, we don't get food. And we have to be back at work by nine the next morning. We are eating whatever, not getting enough sleep and living under the constant threat of termination,' says a second salesperson, 'Rajesh' (name changed). 'A lot of BDAs, mostly in their 20s, have developed physical and mental health issues after joining Byju's.'

Managers control every movement of their team members. There are multiple daily meetings – in the morning to update managers on the number of leads for the day, in the afternoon to update on the number of counselling sessions booked with parents, and then before the close of the day to update on the number of bookings made. Salespeople are often told not to break for lunch or leave for the day until they meet their targets.

They work for 14 hours a day, six days a week. The weekly day off goes in punching in orders taken during the week. If a customer stops responding, the blame falls on the sales rep. In several cases, managers have asked salespeople not to come to work from the next day because a customer hasn't responded.

If someone wants a sick day, they are asked to pop a pill

and come to work instead. Sales reps are often forced to travel over an hour to the office, just so managers can check if they are indeed sick. Only after the manager is satisfied can they go home and apply for medical leave.

All this is done to ensure the entire team hits their stiff allocation of weekly targets. At the time of writing this story, the goal for a salesperson was to bring ₹1.5 lakh in sales a week. For managers who lead a team of 10 salespeople, the target was around ₹7–10 lakh. For the senior managers, it was about ₹70 lakh and so on. If a salesperson failed to meet the target for a while, they were inserted into the performance improvement programme and eventually asked to leave if they kept missing targets.

Things got even worse. In October 2022, the company changed its policy for salespersons. This change suggested that only those who can meet up to 75% of their targets will be put under the performance improvement programme. Those who are not able to meet 50% or above of the monthly target would be asked to leave immediately, which hadn't been the case earlier.

Weekly rankings, with the names of salespeople and their sales figures, are widely shared. In a week in July 2022, one team of 575 salespeople made total sales worth ₹3.74 crore, with the highest individual sale of ₹5.44 lakh. But 263 individuals could not sell anything, dragging down the average sale per rep for the week to ₹65,000.

'You can't imagine the pressure on those 263 individuals. At this point, they will do anything to make a sale, be it fake sale or mis-selling,' says Devaraju N.R., another former salesperson.

To its credit, Byju's has become less tolerant of instances
of fake sales and mis-selling overtime and has even fired the
people involved in such schemes. This is probably because
the incidents tend to eventually surface on social media and
lead to embarrassment.

But the practice is still rampant and often quite
coordinated. Salespeople sometimes put in more than
₹15,000 as down payment from their own pocket to punch
in a sale of, say, ₹2.5 lakh.

Managers ask salespeople in their teams to pool in money,
say ₹500–1,000 each, so they can expedite down payments
and lock in a sale. Such sales are often credited to the person
in the team with the worst numbers. Or they are credited to
team members by turns.

'Sometimes there are even auctions going on in internal
groups, where the highest bidder gets the sale,' says Rajesh,
quoted above.

There are many cases where parents don't sign up after
making the down payment. Most of them don't even know
that they can ask the company to refund the down payment.
Some don't care.

'When the BDA is convinced of a sale, they take the
down payment in the company's account. But in many other
cases, they get the payment in their own accounts,' says
Rajesh. 'Sometimes, this money vanishes without a trace.
Often it is shared with others. The smarter ones keep this
money aside to make down payments in the future.'

Sales staff are told to make sales by whatever means
possible. Makhija gives an example. Once, another
salesperson in the office was on a video conference with a

parent. The demo was done and this person was asking the parent to make the down payment. The parent wanted some time to think and said they didn't have ₹5,000 for the down payment at the time.

So the manager jumped in. He first tried persuasion, then FOMO, even threats. But when nothing worked, he asked the parent if a friend of theirs could loan them ₹5,000 for the down payment. He took the number, called the friend, sent them a UPI link and, thus, made the sale.

Salespeople I spoke with say this level of pressure wasn't there even eight months ago. 'Had the friend also not had the money, the manager would have asked the BDA to make the down payment,' says Makhija.

It is hard to believe that the top management was unaware of such practices. 'But they know the company needs revenue and it is only the managers who can eke out sales,' says the second salesperson.

Many people don't complain because they hope to gain from the system. Those who raise their voice are shunted out and given impossible leads. Many don't complain because they have nowhere else to go.

Byju's hires fresh graduates, gives them a crash course in hard-selling and sets aggressive sales targets. Salespersons, in turn, play fast and loose, giving evasive answers to awkward questions about EMIs, cancellation policy and learning outcomes in order to close a sale.

'They will hire the most desperate salespeople, promising a good salary. But soon, the BDEs will learn that the base salary is only, say, 50% of what they were promised, and the rest will be incentives and bonuses linked to sales,' says Dr Aniruddha Malpani.

Malpani, a doctor by training, is also an angel investor who has been a vocal critic of edtech companies. 'At that point, the BDEs are also stuck. They have to repay their education loan, and support their families. It becomes a question of survival, and it is either them or the consumer.'

The fear of public humiliation if the targets are not met, and the fact that they are surrounded by others who normalize this behaviour, makes matters worse.

———

Employees have asked for changes in work culture and tried to make their voices heard, but in vain. In July 2022, these disgruntled salespersons formed two groups on WhatsApp. One of my sources added me to one of the groups called 'Let's Fight for Rights' where they chatted about the best ways to make their concerns heard. Then managers and other seniors joined the group and started threatening the salespersons. The number of participants quickly depleted and, within a couple of weeks, the groups were shut down. My source, one of the very vocal participants in the group, left the company and moved home to his small town in central India after he was threatened with serious consequences. He rarely leaves home now after what he claims was an attempt on his life.

In October 2022, around the time the company announced that it would cut 2,500 jobs – the actual number of layoffs was reportedly more than 12,000 – another incident of blatant abuse surfaced on social media. Former salesperson Vishal Verma took to LinkedIn to share how he was fired without being notified. In the LinkedIn post, which has since been taken down, Verma recounted his experience of the days leading up to his resignation and the way it was handled, while painting a grim picture of the sales team at Byju's.

In a conversation with me, Verma said he was greeted with expletives by a training manager at a training session when he moved to Bengaluru from Noida in July. His immediate senior kept reminding him that he was Verma's 'f***ing manager and can fire you anytime I want'. This was despite Verma working 12 to 14 hours a day, six days a week, and generating average weekly revenues of ₹3 lakh, which, according to him, was among the best in the company.

When general manager Prithviraj Singh Panesar refused to hear him out, Verma says, he wrote emails to the HR and the top management, which were seldom acknowledged.

'As a result of the emails, I was getting targeted by my manager,' Verma told me. 'One day, after I wrote another email, my manager provoked me to resign, and I did email my resignation in the heat of the moment.'

That was 17 September. Later, Verma withdrew the resignation in subsequent emails, but none of those emails were acknowledged. The resignation was not approved either. In October, when his doctor suggested surgery for the removal of kidney stones, Verma asked for leave or alternatively if he could work from home for three weeks, and promised to meet targets. He got an email from Panesar, saying 'Demands for such long WFH/leaves are not entertained.'

On 4 October, the day before Dussehra, Panesar sent

his team an email saying 'there will be No Leaves approved for 5th Oct. We already have given all BDAs Sun/Mon off which has been detrimental to our revenue efforts.' The next sentence read: 'Please be in office on time. We will be initiating "Absconding procedures" for anyone not in office by 10:30 am.' For the Diwali week, Panesar ensured that his team filled out a form with details such as the date of return and checked the date mentioned on the return ticket as proof before approving one-day leaves.

On 4 October, Verma got an email from associate senior manager Mohit Maurya, asking him to complete his exit formalities. And while he was still following it up with his seniors and the HR team, his employee ID and email account were deactivated.

Byju's did its first mass hiring for sales roles towards the end of 2015, a few months after it raised $25 million from Sequoia Capital India. Hundreds of fresh graduates were hired from colleges like Manipal and Amity. The designation they were offering was BDA, while the role was telecalling. Former salespersons who worked in the company at the time say that while the company was paying higher than industry standards, it didn't tell them that the role was all about telecalling.

'I did get growth, but at the expense of seven-day work weeks with abusive managers,' said 'Amit' (name changed to protect identity), a former sales executive who worked with Byju's in its early days and has closely watched the company since he quit. 'The same culture was then transcended by us as we led teams. We didn't know there was any other culture.'

Especially during 2015–16, Amit says, there was an evident lack of corporate discipline. It was a bunch of really young and inexperienced people leading teams and closing sales and chasing the numbers. For example, there was no structured CBSE/ICSE/state board content and yet the company sold courses claiming the same.

Managers were playing recordings, and asking salespersons to introduce themselves as 'Hi, I'm XYZ, a physics teacher at Byju's and I'm from IIT.' There was an emphasis on the IIT part, which was a lie, and the caller was not working as a teacher, Amit tells me.

'If this is not mis-selling, what is?' Amit asks. 'It is not possible that this pitch happened without the knowledge of the management. But they allowed it for the sake of showing numbers. It went on till things got out of hand.'

The key here is growth numbers. The sole focus at the endless meetings was on numbers. It was all about selling. Processes didn't matter. Neither did ethics. It was all about numbers. In one such meeting, Amit recalls, Raveendran said: 'I am the founder and all you managers are mini-founders of your team.'

The kind of freedom this mindset gave salespeople was immense. Different managers had different strategies and they used the grey area in different ways. But so long as their team met the numbers and the company did well, everything was acceptable. For the salespeople, higher numbers meant better incentives and more money. This gave them power, a sense of invincibility and, in certain cases, a God complex.

'They were not being abusive on a personal basis, but they also didn't realize they were mere pawns in the larger game,' says Amit. This atmosphere and work culture took a toll on the mental health of the BDEs.

When you work day in and day out, pressurize your team, and fire them for not hitting the numbers, you get a false sense of power. But eventually, you see loans are not passing through, parents are calling you, students are calling you and the pressure gets to you. The sense of power evaporates and you might burn out.

There is pressure all the way from the bottom to the very top. For the freshers, there is a daily calling target pressure, a weekly target pressure and a monthly closing pressure. They have to do a minimum of two to two and a half hours of calling, or a loss of pay is likely. Being in the office till late in the evening was normalized because parents are usually free during that period. Interns had to show sales of about ₹5 lakh, which was five to seven times their stipend, to attain permanent status.

Daily meetings with managers would often be humiliating. The managers themselves were also young graduates with barely three to six months of experience, and would give public dressing downs.

There used to be an enforced party culture.

'Managers would convince freshers, who might have other dreams for the future, that Byju's was the place to be. With the money and the freedom it allowed the salespersons, they would explain how it was better than any future job prospect for us,' says Amit. 'What Byju's did was brainwash college grads. It convinced them that they were living a free life in Bengaluru while actually slaving for the company.'

The pressure on the managers was in some respects even higher. A salesperson would get incentives if he completed individual targets and could earn as much as a manager. But for the manager to do well, the team target had to be met. Data suggests that it is impossible to convert more than 2–3% of leads into paying customers and when there is a tough target to meet, there is bound to be mis-selling.

'Byju's has figured out how to survive by using the grey area. You cross enough moral lines to grow, and stay away from a few moral lines to stay in the clear,' says Amit. 'Unethical behaviour in the name of good business has been normalized in edtech due to the likes of Byju's and then later WhiteHat Jr.'

The moral issues faced in this sort of relentless selling goes all the way up to senior manager, and then to vice-president of sales, and finally to the chief operating officer, Mrinal Mohit, or higher.

There is no one in the system solving for issues faced by the student/parent after a certain point, because of the sole focus on numbers. When a complaint comes from a parent, the bottom of the pyramid, the salesperson who made the call, is thrown under the bus. Since the parents only spoke with the caller, they only have their number. The caller becomes the easiest target if a parent is unhappy with Byju's.

'Even now, when parental complaints increased so much that they went to the authorities, instead of taking accountability as senior leaders at CXO levels, they find it easy to pick out the intern and fire them,' says Amit. 'The only thing that has changed from then and now is that now they get some training before starting work and things are somewhat more streamlined. But the lives of salespersons are still as bad.'

———

'Some of the freshers live in the same building where I do,' says Makhija. 'When they return home at night, they look like zombies. There are no parties. They don't have any life. They work and they sleep. Worse, at the end of the month, most of them are told that the company can't hire them because of the lower volume of business.'

Towards the end of 2022, the company tried to change its sales model to what it calls inside sales to cut down costs as well as complaints of mis-selling. Inside sales is the practice of calling customers over the phone or through video conferencing platforms like Zoom instead of making home visits. Field visits are costlier and have greater scope for fake sales since the company can't record or audit what the salesperson promises the customer at their home. Inside sales allows everything to be recorded and audited. Here, costs are low, but so are the conversion rates.

Two questions arise. One, why would a company that was built on the back of foot soldiers suddenly abandon its sales strategy? Two, did it help?

To answer the second question first, it didn't. Another sales executive, 'Shiva' (name changed), who was still with Byju's when we spoke, told me that resorting to inside sales hasn't helped. It has only made conversions harder. Given a rising number of layoffs – we will talk about that in a bit – the pressure on the existing salespersons to make the numbers has increased.

The answer to the why lies in the huge customer acquisition cost that makes unit economics unsustainable in the long run, especially in a market where capital is now scarce and expensive.

———

Unit economics is wonky at Byju's. The company has been burning cash for years, but no one talks about it because (a) it had been able to raise money fairly easily till 2021, and (b) it had been claiming to generate profit in the core business, until the horrendous results of FY21 exposed that claim for fiction.

Let's try and understand Byju's unit economics for sales, starting with figures and information from the fiscal 2019–20 earnings declaration and other resources in the public domain.

Using 2019–20 as the base year helps us gain clarity because it was the last year before the big bang acquisitions of WhiteHat Jr and Aakash, and we can avoid mixing up sales from those verticals.

These figures are admittedly a few years old and the pandemic did change the dynamics of edtech, but even with those caveats, the core business – selling supplementary education courses for subjects such as maths and chemistry for schoolchildren – has not fundamentally changed. The sales model only changed in end-2022 (FY22–23) when they moved to inside sales.

Take a look at the table below; it's a little complicated, so we'll run through an explanation of what you see.

Average Units Sold per Salespersons per Month	6
Unit Cost (w/o GST)	₹55,085
Gross Monthly Sales	₹345,934
Monthly Sales Net of Returns @ 20%	₹276,893
Less Sales Cost (including salaries)	₹113,421
Net Monthly Revenues	₹163,471
Less Marketing Cost	₹65,000
Less Product Cost	₹41,000
Margin (₹)	₹57,471
Margin (%)	20.76%

Salespeople at Byju's sell an average of around six units per month. Note this is a weighted average – some high performers sell more and some average performers sell less. The average ticket size net of GST is around ₹55,000 for a two- or three-year programme. Average returns and cancellations are somewhere upwards of 20%, but we'll stick to a conservative 20% estimate.

Net of returns, the weighted average sale per salesperson is about ₹2.76 lakh.

Now, consider costs. The average salary of a BDA is ₹7 lakh, or around ₹58,000 a month. Incentives are 20% of the fixed salary, i.e. ₹1.4 lakh a year; the actual bonus paid out could range from 50% of this to 150%, depending on an individual's performance. The cost to company is between ₹64,000 and ₹75,000 a month per salesperson. Add finance costs at 5% (most purchases are financed) and travel costs, assuming the salesperson converts one in four visits. The weighted average cost works out to about ₹1.13 lakh in monthly costs per salesperson. So the net earnings, after cost of sales, per salesperson in a month is about ₹1.6 lakh.

Now deduct costs of the product – tablets, SD cards, books, shipping, etc., which comes to about ₹41,000 a month, per salesperson. Finally, deduct lead generation costs (ads/promotions) at an estimated 25% of sales. Net revenue per salesperson is a little over ₹57,000 a month. This ballpark estimate maybe on the generous side of the gross margin; the assumptions are conservative with some costs, such as the cost of the product and the cost of lead generation.

This is about a 20% margin for the core business. Managerial overheads, according to industry estimates, is also about 20% of sales, which effectively wipes out the net revenue per salesperson.

When other costs like office overheads, tech infrastructure, online tutoring in case of online classes, mentor cost for doubt solving, sales support, etc., are taken into account, there would be significant net losses. This calculation gels with the huge losses reported in Byju's published financials, which we look at in a later chapter.

The impact – as many observers have pointed out – has been even worse than apparent from the reported numbers. Byju's used to recognize all the revenue upfront for each unit programme sold right at the time of the initial sale. But its programmes are mostly multi-year and the cost of servicing is expensed as it comes up, year after year.

Long story short, the reported numbers suggest the economics of the core K–12 business don't work. The company would need to bump up unit sales per salesperson by a large margin, which doesn't seem to be easy. Growing volumes by adding sales staff and spending more on lead generation won't help with the margins.

After the company switched to inside sales, the costs came down. But revenues also fell drastically, creating additional pressures for the sales teams.

———

I will leave this topic of sales with a strategy that Devaraju described as one of the tricks used to identify potential customers. He recalled the case of one single parent from northern Karnataka. Managers, he says, have been asking them to focus on single parents, especially single mothers.

'They are easier sells for two reasons. One, a large number of them are living a tough life and would do anything to make the lives of their children better; and two, they don't have the time or the resources to check the efficacy of the product,' Devaraju says.

This particular parent, in her late 30s, was uneducated, and worked in the informal sector, earning around ₹300–₹400 daily – a typical 'low-hanging fruit'. Her child was in high school then. The sale was easy and so was the loan process. Everyone was happy. Until the day the first loan instalment was debited from the parent's account.

She realized she couldn't afford it. She didn't know how to cancel the product either. So she called up Devaraju.

'She wanted a refund. I assured her that I would look into the matter,' says Devaraju. 'In reality, I had no power.'

So he went to the manager and narrated the event. 'He told me that my job ended when I punched in the sale,' says the salesperson. 'He told me to block this parent's number, move on and focus on the next sale.'

Devaraju blocked the mother's number but didn't have the heart to make another sale after this. Within 10 days, he resigned.

7

Offside

Byju's shocked edtech watchers once again in February 2022, when the company announced that it would launch 500 tuition centres across 200 cities by the end of the year at a cost of $200 million and enrol 1 million students.

The company had reportedly been toying with the idea since July 2021. Byju's Tuition Centre was run as a pilot across 80 centres and then launched towards the end of the year. This was another left-of-centre move, considering the whole world had been betting on the online education model and Byju's itself claimed online registrations and subscriptions had jumped significantly during the lockdown.

Mohit told YourStory that the company was not 'going from digital to offline. We are, in fact, taking digital to offline ... there is a set of parents who like online but still believe in the need of physical elements in learning. This is catering to this set of customers, who want a physical element in addition to the online teaching.'

Unacademy, Vendantu, PW (earlier called Physics Wallah) – every edtech player worth its salt – followed suit.

The companies all explained the move to offline as the most natural progression of their respective businesses in the post-pandemic world.

'Our experiential touchpoints have seen tremendous response from learners, many of whom have also expressed the need for in-person learning from the best educators,' Unacademy co-founder and CEO Gaurav Munjal said in a press statement after announcing in May that the company will start coaching centres.

This was BIG.

Let's take a step back and rewind. The promise of edtech companies was to democratize education. They were going to be the alternative to the expensive and bloated tuition and coaching centres. Edtech companies were supposed to use technology to go remote, change the shape of pedagogy, make learning holistic and fun, and thus take education out of the confines of four walls of conventional classrooms, making it accessible to all.

Edtech start-ups raised billions of dollars by promising to fulfil that dream. The segment has raised more than $10 billion cumulatively since 2016. This money was supposed to help start-ups create digital platforms. Now the same companies were saying that online education can go only so far? Despite the experience of nearly two years of lockdown when everything moved online? Why?

When the lockdown began and online seemed to be the only way forward for learning, everyone and their uncles, including me at The Morning Context, had written epitaphs for the offline coaching business. Move online or die, the industry watchers said. But now the same companies that once pioneered online teaching and swore that they wanted to kill coaching centres were now saying, 'Wait, hold on, we need physical coaching centres.'

Indian edtech was witnessing a seismic shift again. There was no adverse investor reaction, which was surprising since the investors had bought the online story. But now edtech companies changed the narrative, saying hybrid is the future because (a) online can't replace schools, and (b) there is pandemic fatigue. Investors bought into that shift in focus.

By the middle of the calendar year 2022, it was clear that the edtech party was over. After two years of growth at a blistering pace, the wheels were slowly coming off the edtech story.

The reversal started in February 2022 with Lido Learning. This was a three-year-old online tutorial platform that taught maths, science, coding and English to children between kindergarten and grade 12. Lido Learning shut down operations and asked nearly 1,200 employees to resign during a virtual townhall meeting. There was a financial crisis, founder Sahil Sheth told them. That was it.

On 9 February, the day after the town hall, the entire sales team, nearly 1,000 of them, was fired via a mass email. The operations team was dissolved. Teachers were told to quit. One minute, they had jobs. The next minute, they didn't.

In a matter of minutes, thousands of students and their parents – many of whom had taken multi-year courses on EMIs – were stuck with their futures tied to a dodo, an extinct edtech. This was just weeks before final exams for the academic year. Hundreds of students and parents took to social media. The India Edtech Consortium – an autonomous self-governing body created a little over a month before to regulate the actions of its member edtech companies – faced a crisis.

The optics got even worse than the bald outcome of shutting down a business and leaving thousands of consumers and employees in the lurch. Even as the IEC was scrambling to find a home for Lido Learning's students, and more than a thousand employees were anxiously hoping they would receive their final salaries, Sheth was nowhere to be found. In September 2022, when Lido Learning filed for bankruptcy, my sources sent me a bunch of screenshots from social media, indicating Sheth was travelling and partying in the days leading to the bankruptcy.

Callousness apart, Lido Learning wasn't the only company in trouble. The truth is that the industry had been showing signs of overheating for a while and it was just a matter of time before things went south for other edtechs.

Vedantu fired 624 employees, nearly 10% of its workforce, in May. Over 800 people resigned from WhiteHat Jr when asked to relocate in the same month. FrontRow, a celebrity-focused online learning and community platform, sacked 145 employees by email around the same time.

Between January and June 2022, Unacademy gradually laid off over 1,000 people. 'Winter is here. Tech stocks globally are crashing and burning due to tighter monetary policies and rising interest rates. We are looking at a time where funding will dry up for at least 12–18 months. Some people are predicting that this might last 24 months. We must adapt,' Unacademy's co-founder and CEO Gaurav Munjal said in an email to employees in May.

In June, Udayy, a two-year-old start-up that provided an immersive learning platform for children between kindergarten and grade 8, shut down operations and laid off its entire workforce.

Edtech might have been the worst hit, but the crisis there mirrored how things were panning out across the larger domains of IT and IT-enabled services and digital start-ups. Start-ups like Furlenco, Trell, OkCredit, Cars24, Meesho, Blinkit and MFine, laid off thousands of people in India alone in the first five months of calendar 2022. It was the same elsewhere in the world. Layoffs in tech start-ups worldwide surged to a record level, indicating a more challenging climate ahead. Macroeconomic and geopolitical challenges hurt economies from Shanghai to San Francisco.

Through the pandemic, central banks around the world, including the US Federal Reserve, kept monetary policy loose and maintained record-low policy rates. This created excess liquidity in the market at a point of time when output was down and global supply chains were disrupted. This pushed inflation up because there was a lot of money chasing very little in the way of goods and services.

Hundreds of billions of dollars were pumped into internet businesses across the world. Eventually, to rein in the inflation monster it had created, the Fed started to hike policy rates and announced that it might raise interest rates multiple times in 2022 to squeeze out excess liquidity. This set the cat among the pigeons as other central banks also followed suit and money supply tightened.

Investors started dumping technology stocks, which resulted in higher volatility. Tech stocks across the world got hammered. There was a bloodbath on the Nasdaq – the tech-heavy index lost 15% between November 2021 and January 2022. Tighter money supply also hurt the venture capital market and led to a funding winter for start-ups. Investors moved away from risky assets to hard-currency government bonds. This theme ran on through the year and at the time of writing this book (August 2023), global inflation is still high and so are policy rates.

Adding to this was the recessionary fear, stoked by rising inflation and slowing growth. And if that wasn't enough, a full-fledged war, which had been simmering since Russia's annexation of Crimea in 2014, began as Russia invaded Ukraine on 24 February 2022.

A retail investor told me he had invested about $5 million in tech stocks in the US in 2020, and saw his net asset value jump to $50 million in a year and then plunge to $500,000 in the blink of an eye during the tech stock rout. Things turned so bad that VC funds started warning their portfolio companies about an impending funding crunch. The Menlo Park, California, headquartered Sequoia Capital, for example, sent a 52-slide presentation to its portfolio companies, describing the situation – the triad of turbulent financial markets, inflationary pressures and geopolitical conflict – as a 'crucible moment' for uncertainty and change. It warned founders of an impending funding crunch. Several other VC funds followed suit.

Consequently, VC/PE investments in India's edtech sector recorded a nearly 50% decline in 2022 over the previous year. The tide was going out. A funding winter set in.

It would still have been acceptable if the demand for online learning had grown steadily or, at the very least, stayed intact. But with the pandemic subsiding and the world reopening, there was a drastic fall in the number of students studying online. The pandemic-induced hypothesis that once learners moved online, they would stick with it, has now been proved wrong. No one was ready for this exodus, least of all the edtech companies and the investors who had bet on online learning staying sticky.

Edtech start-ups had thought the shift in consumer behaviour was permanent. Irreversible. They had bet heavily on this hypothesis over the last two years.

During that period, the lines between various segments had also blurred. Every start-up that could, got into every possible segment, especially into K–12. Given more than a quarter of a billion learners in that demographic cohort in India, it was the hottest segment during the pandemic.

Eruditus entered K–12 with the acquisition of iD Tech in the US. Unacademy had acquired Mastree. Then there was Byju's, which wanted all roads to lead to, well, Byju's. The acquisition of Toppr had given it a clear lead in the K–12 segment. Then the company acquired Aakash Education and Gradeup to get into test-prep. The acquisition of Great Learning gave it a firm footing in higher education and upskilling. All these start-ups hired freely while the VC funding was easily accessible. As lockdowns eased up and educational institutes reopened, students rushed back to schools and colleges.

In India, the education ministry's National Achievement Survey (NAS) 2021, which was conducted to assess the learning outcomes and health of the education system, made a surprising assessment. It reported that 78% of the 3.4 million students across 720 districts who participated in the survey found remote learning 'burdensome with a lot of assignments'. Four out of five participants said they had learnt better at school with the help of peers and at least 38% of students faced serious difficulties in learning at home.

Naturally, the unlock impacted the K–12 segment the most since that was actually the biggest group of signups. It forced edtech entrepreneurs to wake up and smell the coffee. They had been caught off-guard.

If you look at the evolution of edtech in India over the last few years, you will see that beyond changing the medium of delivery, edtech start-ups haven't been able to change much else. What they teach is only a digitized version of the same school and coaching centre material. They tried to play around with the idea of students learning at their own pace, but most haven't been able to prove outcomes from this approach. Unfortunately, parents are only concerned with results and grades and they believe coaching centres have a better chance of delivering those outcomes. Edtech start-ups never gained the same credibility – they were only seen as the best of the available options during the pandemic when offline teaching was impossible.

The benefits of peer learning and the impact of pandemic

fatigue apart, there was also an overwhelming realization that online education cannot engage students like physical centres do.

'When my two children are attending classes online, they are also chatting with people, browsing through social media and watching Korean dramas simultaneously,' an expert who has been tracking education from inside and outside the industry for years told me. 'There are a lot of distractions and no real accountability to learning.' In comparison, schools and coaching centres have fewer distractions. This was a huge draw and a USP for parents who looked for the physical option once it became available again.

The schools' gain was edtech's loss. This wasn't just about a liquidity crunch, though that constricted resources for edtechs. It was behavioural and it was way bigger.

As students and parents turned their backs on online learning, the edtech industry figured out that it had burnt billions of investors' dollars on a false premise. During the pandemic, edtechs were so focused on growth, they forgot the basics. Now, they were stranded with no options other than rationalizing their workforces and reducing costs to try and survive. Sadly, not every edtech survived.

'As the kids went back to school, we faced roadblocks in growing the original model of online, live learning. We evaluated multiple different strategies and adjacent pivots. However, none of them were promising enough. After a lot of deliberation, we decided that it's better to shut down the business than to spend more time and capital on it. Our investors, team members and customers have been very supportive,' Udayy co-founder Saumya Yadav said in a statement after shutting down operations.

Gaurav Munjal, the co-founder and CEO of Unacademy, told me during an interview that his company built its K–12 product because of the FOMO.

'. . . we never thought of doing K–12. Somewhere down the journey, people started comparing us with Byju's. We saw WhiteHat Jr and others doing well, and we felt we needed to play the market. We were struck with FOMO,' he told me. 'That's when we bought a majority stake in Mastree. But we didn't know the market. We thought we could crack it just like we cracked test prep. And we were wrong.'

K–12 is inherently different from test-prep or higher education. The K–12 products are used by children but are sold to parents. There is a mismatch of expectations from the very beginning. The sale depends on the salesperson's ability to create FOMO. Nobody had figured out how to exploit this as well as Byju's. Unsurprisingly, it didn't work for Unacademy. The company had to shut down its K–12 business.

———

Byju's was feeling the pinch even more. This will reflect in the company's financials for the period whenever it decides to release the earnings reports. It had to resort to cost-cutting and downsizing. But for the second time in two years, it seemed the company had been able to predict the direction of the trend and change course accordingly, making it the first edtech to go offline.

The offline business could not only give it a lifeline but could also become a second engine for growth. Aakash was having its best year ever after the unlock. Students rushed back to Kota as soon as the city reopened. Then in May 2022, Bodhi Tree Systems, an investment platform backed by James Murdoch and Uday Shankar, invested $600 million in the Kota-based test-prep company ALLEN Career Institute. This was the first investment of note in an offline test-prep company since the Blackstone Group's investment in Aakash Educational Services in 2019.

Byju's doubled down on the tuition centre business. It hired Himanshu Bajaj, former head of consumer and retail practice for Asia at global consultancy firm Kearney, to lead Byju's Tuition Centres, and brought in professionals with years of experience to build the business.

Edtech founders told me this was the right move since online was anyway a stopgap arrangement due to the pandemic and offline was where the sticky margins were. Everyone followed suit.

To hedge against a cash crunch in the future, Byju's was also going all out to raise all the money it could from wherever it could. Venture capital, debt, selling trade receivables – you name it and the company was doing it. Raveendran left no stone unturned to raise capital and boost the company's cash position. He had to. He had promised to take the company public soon.

But that isn't to say Byju's was finding the fundraising easy.

In March 2022, Raveendran announced his company would raise around $800 million in a fresh round of funding.

He also announced that he would invest half of this amount himself. Around the same time, he started Byjus Investments Pvt. Ltd. This company, and Raveendran in his own capacity, raised money from individuals, family offices and institutions in the form of debt and debentures and then invested the money in the holding company Think & Learn.

In May 2022, there was news that Byju's was in talks with banks, including Morgan Stanley and JPMorgan Chase, to raise more than $1 billion in debt for acquisition financing. The company was said to be in talks to buy either the textbook rental start-up, Chegg or 2U, the parent of online learning platform edX.

That money never came in. Those acquisitions never happened.

8

Unforced Errors

2022 was a year of reckoning, a turning point for Byju's in more ways than one. After a hiring spree during the pandemic years of 2020 and 2021, this was a year of mass layoffs. Also, for the first time in its history, the company was forced to change the way it recognized revenues, which resulted in a record loss for FY20–21, as Byju's watchers discovered when the company released its earnings report for the 12 months ending 31 March 2021, with a delay of 18 months, in September 2022. The same year, for the first time, there were phantom fundraises at Byju's – tranches of funding that were announced but never arrived. Also, 2022 was the year the company came close to a public listing, which ultimately wasn't to be.

———

I sent an email. The response was chaotic.

On the evening of Sunday, 30 January 2022, within an hour after I had sent an email with six questions, I received a call from Byju's, asking if I wanted to talk to a senior company official to understand the background of the story I was working on.

My digging indicated that Byju's plan to explore a public listing in the US through a special purpose acquisition company (SPAC), first reported by Bloomberg in December 2021, had gone off-track. The questions I had sent were in line with my findings and I needed the company's responses on record. So, when the request came for an off-the-record chat, I politely declined.

A second call came within half an hour, asking if I wanted to talk off the record with Anita Kishore, an engineer-turned-teacher-turned-strategist, who was at the time the head of finance and chief strategy officer at the company. She was also at the forefront as the face of Byju's global ambitions. As the head of finance, she, I was told, could give me the right perspective so I could write a balanced story. Again, I declined to have an off-the-record chat.

On the dot at the 30-minute mark after I had concluded the second call, I received another call. This time, I was told that it was Raveendran who wanted to talk. It would be the first time we spoke since I started writing about education technology in 2020. This, I could not pass up.

So there we were, chatting away on a WhatsApp video call for over 90 minutes. During the call, Raveendran tried to convince me that the SPAC was on track, his tone swinging between confusion, mild irritation and what sounded like veiled intimidation.

The December 2021 Bloomberg report said Byju's was in talks with Michael Dell's MSD Acquisition Corp. and

Altimeter Capital Management for a possible SPAC merger.
It also said that the company was the farthest along in
working out an agreement with Michael Klein's Churchill
Capital.

A SPAC is a publicly traded shell company created with
the sole purpose of effecting a merger with a private company
to help the private company go public. Investors – generally
hedge funds or institutional investors – come together, pool
in money from sponsors, identify a good company and help
take it public. It is a faster, more convenient way to get to
a public listing than via an IPO. It bypasses the process
of due diligence that is required to take an operational
private business public. Investors get a quick return on good
companies and companies that may have taken time or had
trouble going public in the US get a quick, hassle-free listing.

As per the preliminary terms, the Bloomberg report said,
Byju's would raise about $4 billion at a $48 billion valuation.
It also suggested that a deal could be announced in January
2022. There was a caveat, though. As is common with all such
negotiations, either of the parties could opt out of the deal.

Nevertheless, this was a big moment, not only for India's
nascent education technology sector but the entire internet
economy. Here was India's largest edtech company, defying
the law of gravity, allaying the fears of overheating, and
growing even bigger in terms of valuations and getting a $4
billion infusion into the bargain.

The SPAC was, however, not only the next step in the
natural progression of Byju's, it was a necessity.

Between January 2020 – right before the Covid-19
outbreak in India – and the Bloomberg report in December

[handwritten annotation: summary of valuation changes]

2021, Byju's valuation soared from $8 billion to around $21 billion on the back of more than $3.1 billion raised in venture capital funding. This is the kind of exponential growth dreams are made of. But it was also <u>inexplicable</u> and <u>irrational</u>. Buoyed by investor interest and then the pandemic boost, the company went on a shopping spree. Byju's acquired 11 companies, including 3 in the US, for nearly $3 billion, according to data from Venture Intelligence. A hiring spree followed.

As a result, Byju's needed more funds. Not only to continue operating at such a massive scale but also to fuel future acquisitions. For a company that grew on a diet of private capital, this was a moment of truth. Any late-stage company with high valuation finds it hard to access private capital anymore in the quantities required. Also, investors were tightening their belts to hedge against the volatility in global markets prompted by the US Federal Reserve's policy stance.

As the Fed tightened its monetary policy, and tech valuations plummeted, Byju's realized that a public listing was the only way to unlock value and give existing shareholders an exit opportunity as well as raise cash for future growth. Raveendran knew this for sure. He had been talking about a potential public listing since April 2021.

The question now was, where would Byju's do an IPO? The depth of the public markets to raise funds and get good valuations is much more in the US than in India or anywhere else for that matter.

Given Byju's steep valuation and the substantial amount it was trying to raise, the chances of a public offer succeeding were better in the US than in India. But there was a big roadblock – Indian companies are not allowed direct foreign listing. In March 2022, the Indian government mothballed its previous policy directive to allow Indian companies to list overseas. The policy U-turn was taken with the belief that there is enough depth in the local capital markets, with the view that the move will bolster them. Whatever the logic, the policy meant that Byju's couldn't just directly list on an American exchange. But a SPAC listed in the US could buy a private Indian company without contravening any regulations.

That is how a SPAC merger emerged as the best-case scenario for the company. First, it was faster and more convenient than the traditional IPO route. Second, it would hedge against short-term market volatility. Third, and most important, it was pretty much the only legal way for Byju's to tap the US capital markets. The SPAC merger, in short, was a lifeline for the company.

Raveendran's irritation during our call, therefore, was understandable. My reporting had indicated that the SPAC plan was off because of the crash in global markets, including the US. Due to the rout in tech stocks, investor attitude had changed, one source told me, in a matter of a few weeks.

Because of the crash, the IPO window had closed, another source told me. It was so bad, he said, that there was a very slim chance of a big tech IPO in all of 2022. A third source indicated that the deal got stuck on valuation. Things were fine one day and then negotiations broke down after the market crashed.

Over the video call, however, Raveendran told me the

information I had was misleading at best, and incorrect at worst. He questioned the motivation of the sources, the veracity of their claims and our vetting process of their assertions. He shared his screen and skimmed through WhatsApp chats with multiple investors, always ensuring that the fonts were never big enough to read with the naked eye. He told me he had multiple term sheets and promised he could get investors on a live call to clear my doubts, despite it being a Sunday morning in the US. He didn't make any of those calls.

But I continued to have reservations and we stood by our story. Our sources were credible and authentic. The publicly available data showed that the tech sector had gone bearish. Moreover, nothing Raveendran said was admissible because the conversation was off the record. The company also refused to respond on record or even acknowledge it had received the email. The term sheets Raveendran was referring to were just that, term sheets, a non-binding agreement outlining the basic terms and conditions of the investment. I could not see any concrete commitment by investors.

Raveendran also promised an announcement, latest by the end of February, and a deal to be signed by the end of March.

Nothing happened. Days turned into weeks and then months. No announcement happened. The chances of a SPAC merger kept diminishing with each passing day. The only person who wouldn't admit it even off the record was Raveendran.

The Morning Context revisited the SPAC issue in June. We spoke to SPAC experts. We dug through the numbers.

Data showed that despite being around since the 1980s, SPACs had never become mainstream. The reason was that investor perception of these vehicles was largely negative.

But in 2019, the construct made a comeback with two big-bang mergers in the form of Draftkings and Virgin Galactic. Soon the SPAC became a craze.

According to data from SPACInsider, in 2019, 59 SPACs were created, with $13 billion invested; in 2020, there were 248 SPACs, with $83 billion invested; in 2021, there were 613 SPACs, with $162 billion invested. It came to a point when too many SPACs were competing for too few targets. This was during the era of high liquidity, of course. Once the Fed tightened money supply, in 2022, only 86 SPACs were created, with an investment of $13 billion.

SPAC Transactions over the Years

IPO Date	IPO Count	Gross Public Proceeds ($Mn)	Avg IPO Size ($Mn)
1 January 2023	25	4,227.96	169.12
1 January 2022	86	13,430.70	156.17
1 January 2021	613	162,502.57	265.09
1 January 2020	248	83,379.52	336.21
1 January 2019	59	13,608.31	230.65
1 January 2018	46	10,751.94	233.74
1 January 2017	34	10,048.46	295.54
1 January 2016	13	3,499.16	269.17
1 January 2015	20	3,902.45	195.12
1 January 2014	12	1,749.75	145.81

IPO Date	IPO Count	Gross Public Proceeds ($Mn)	Avg IPO Size ($Mn)
1 January 2013	10	1,455.27	145.53
1 January 2012	9	490.50	54.50
1 January 2011	15	1,081.53	72.10
1 January 2010	7	502.52	71.79
1 January 2009	1	36.00	36.00

Source: https://www.spacinsider.com/data/stats

Sumeet Mehra, managing director at PTK Acquisition Corp. (SPAC) in the San Francisco Bay Area, told me this: 'In 2020–21, when money was cheap and the market was flush with liquidity, there were on average two SPAC IPOs every day. But then the markets turned.'

When we spoke around June 2022, Mehra told me there were about 600 SPACs that didn't have a deal. Many of these stood the risk of getting liquidated because SPACs have a maximum life of 24 months. So, if a shell company can't identify a target within 24 months, it will be liquidated. This means sponsors will lose their risk capital – the money spent on non-refundable payments to bankers, lawyers and accountants, etc., to cover operating expenses. So, it is in the interest of sponsors to keep moving to different targets in case one deal falls through. Considering nothing at all has happened since the SPAC plan was announced, it was safe to assume that Byju's SPAC plans were long dead and buried.

We received a tip in June 2022. Somebody informed The Morning Context that a venture capital firm with close ties to a 'yogi' had promised but not invested in Byju's. A few more phone calls later, we had a name: Sumeru Ventures.

Byju's announced in March 2022 that it had raised $800 million from Sumeru Ventures, Vitruvian Partners and BlackRock, at a valuation of $22 billion. The round was led by Raveendran putting in $400 million. While Raveendran was able to stitch together $400 million in debt from high-net-worth individuals, and money came in from the other two big investors, the commitment of Sumeru Ventures, around ₹1,300 crore, hadn't come in yet. Worse, we were told that there was a very slim chance of it coming through. The entire episode merited a closer look.

So I dug deeper for whatever information was available about Sumeru Ventures and, in the process, encountered red flag after red flag. First up, we learnt that one of the investors in the round had initiated a probe into Sumeru Ventures by the US corporate investigation and risk consulting firm, Kroll. This in itself is unusual – an investor investigating another investor. The investigation had apparently found serious discrepancies with the company. It was enough to keep digging.

Between January and April 2022, four companies – food delivery start-up Swiggy, healthcare platform GOQii, Byju's, and VerSe Innovation, the operator of news aggregator Dailyhunt and the short-video app Josh – announced fundraises in which Sumeru Ventures was a prominent investor.

After rummaging through hundreds of documents

downloaded from the Ministry of Corporate Affairs website, I realized that not a single penny from Sumeru Ventures had landed in any of the four companies.

The Sumeru Ventures website described the firm as a $1 billion global technology fund 'actively investing across all stages in innovative companies, utilizing transformational technologies like Artificial Intelligence, Machine Learning, Blockchain to create impact'. But there were no details on the companies it had funded over the years. The website didn't have a portfolio section. The company was launched in 2018 but it had made no investments in four years. Its blog hadn't been updated since 2020. Same for its LinkedIn page. By the time of going to press, the website had vanished.

Now, VC funds tend to wear their investments, especially successful ones, as a badge of honour. They highlight their most successful or most promising investments prominently on their website. These become markers of their acumen and indicators of their success. Potential investors in a VC look at the portfolio before they commit funds. But the Sumeru Ventures website didn't have a portfolio section at all.

There were two people managing the fund – Jatin Chaurasia and Saumen Chakraborty. Neither has had a stellar career, or much apparent experience in investing, or managing such large funds.

Chakraborty, who carries his Joey Tempest locks over a pair of jeans or a suit with equal ease, is said to have over 30 years' experience in the 'global information technology industry' and has been associated with 'some of the world's largest fortune 500 companies like DEC, IBM, Quadrant II Technologies, Microsoft, and Hughes'. But his LinkedIn profile doesn't list any work history before Sumeru Ventures.

A cursory search on the company information platform Zauba Corp shows Chakraborty is associated with multiple companies as a director. Two companies, Intelsys Technologies Pvt. Ltd and Intellisys Technologies & Research Pvt. Ltd, are of particular interest.

Intelsys, incorporated in Kolkata in 1999, is a manufacturing company. It doesn't seem to have a website or a contact number. Its listed address is Elgin Chambers on Ashutosh Mukherjee Road in Kolkata – a huge commercial complex that houses many businesses. Here's where it gets even more interesting: data from corporate research firm Corpository shows there are at least two pending cases against the company – one in the Calcutta High Court related to income tax and the other in the Gurugram District Court under the Negotiable Instruments Act.

Intellisys, a group company incorporated in 2007, shares the same Elgin Chambers address. Its website doesn't exist anymore. Corpository data shows this company has over 90 cases of default, starting in 2017, against it. It is facing nine open cases in multiple high courts, six open cases in various district courts, two open cases in the National Company Law Tribunal and one pending case at the Debts Recovery Tribunal in Kolkata.

A lawyer who has followed Chakraborty's journey told me that such a high number of cases against a software company was unprecedented.

'There are money suits, cases of bounced cheques and IBC cases filed against him, Chandrani Chakraborty and Intellisys,' he said. IBC is short for the Insolvency and Bankruptcy Code. 'It seems like loans worth ₹50 crore were taken and then defaulted. A software company without any assets doesn't take ₹50 crore in loans, nor does it default. Also, a software company facing so many money suits is not normal.'

In documents filed with the BSE in December 2021, Axis Bank alleged 'cheating and forgery' by Intellisys Technologies and Research to the tune of ₹21.75 crore.

One venture capitalist who has interacted with Chakraborty had this to say: 'Mr Saumen Chakraborty is a very, very interesting character. His company Intellisys is a sham and has no operations to speak of. He tried very hard to attract government grants. Now he spends most of his time in the US.'

Looking at all the details we gleaned, it seems strange to have somebody with a track record like Chakraborty in charge of a $1 billion fund that intends to invest in start-ups.

Chakraborty has since founded Elysium Ventures, a venture fund focused on AI and deep tech. Here too, his conduct has been unusual. In January 2023, a consultant from Dubai reached out to me to ask about Chakraborty. In his attempt to raise money, Chakraborty had been promoting himself as the global ambassador for the University of Berkeley and someone who 'launched IBM in India'. At the time of going to press, Chakraborty's LinkedIn page had no trace of Sumeru Ventures. The website of Elysium Ventures has a login feature for investors. Without a login, one can't access any information on the team, its portfolio, and so on.

Chaurasia, the other managing director of the fund, did a couple of stints as an analyst in Seattle before heading to Sumeru Inc., which provides technology consulting and digital solutions, in Los Angeles. He has been with the company since 2007 and is now its president. He was formerly the CEO of The Art of Living Digital and joined Sumeru Ventures in February 2019.

Neither managing director has the usual VC background. Neither has any proven track record in investing. Both Chakraborty and Chaurasia, as well as Sumeru Ventures, have indelible links with spiritual leader Sri Sri Ravi Shankar and his Art of Living Foundation.

Chaurasia was introduced to the Art of Living Foundation in 2002 as a volunteer. According to his LinkedIn profile, he is 'one of the few individuals who has worked at different levels of the Art of Living's global network and is known and respected within the community for his work through Sumeru Inc. and Art of Living Digital'. He has also 'extensively traveled with Gurudev Sri Sri Ravishankar over the years'. In 2018, he became the global CEO of Art of Living Digital, the global IT vertical of the Art of Living Foundation.

Chakraborty, too, has a Ravi Shankar connection. The Intellisys Technologies website has photos from a visit to the guru for a 'technology demonstration', in one of which Chakraborty is seen touching Ravi Shankar's feet. There are other occasions too where Chakraborty has been spotted with the spiritual leader.

I reached out to 20 people in the start-up ecosystem from Bengaluru to the Bay Area to find out more about the fund. But no one seems to have heard about either the fund or its managing directors. One entrepreneur helped me find a clearer connection between Sumeru Ventures and the Art of Living Foundation.

'Their address points to a church [the Second Church of Christ, Scientist], the same place where the Art of Living seems to be registered,' said the entrepreneur. 'That's not a business address, and I would be wary of any bank accepting that.'

The landing page of Sumeru Ventures opened with a big photo of Ravi Shankar. On multiple pages, the link with the spiritual leader was very obvious. Its address, 948 W Adams Blvd., Los Angeles, CA 90007, is the Second Church of Christ, Scientist, a building that was acquired by Sri Sri Ravi Shankar's Art of Living Foundation and is, today, the Art of Living Center, Los Angeles. The connection was clear as daylight. We went ahead and published the story.

Two things happened after that. First, Ravi Shankar's secretary reached out to The Morning Context, saying '…Gurudev Sri Sri Ravi Shankar is not in any way associated with Sumeru Ventures. Gurudev's picture in the article is misleading. We ask that you correct the article and remove all references to Gurudev.'

I asked him why the address listed on Sumeru Ventures's website was '948 W Adams Blvd., Los Angeles, CA 90007'. His response: 'The address that you mentioned is a complex with office and living space. They used to rent there.'

Second, Sumeru Ventures scrubbed its website clean of any mention of Art of Living or this address. But here's the thing about the internet. Nothing dies on the World Wide Web; even when you think you have buried something at the bottom of the Pacific, the information always flows to the top. One has to only keep on looking.

how to find old deleted web pages?

Archived versions of the Sumeru Ventures website show the address and pages with references such as, 'Through its partnership with the Art of Living Foundation, Sumeru Ventures also has expertise to offer support to help entrepreneurs with their mental and spiritual health so that they can reach their full potential.'

There is more. At the time of writing this story for The Morning Context, I took a quick look at the domain name system (DNS) entries for Sumeru Ventures and Sumeru Inc., which showed the websites were still being managed by Namit Behl who had an artofliving.org webmail address. Behl's LinkedIn profile listed him as a solutions architect at Sumeru Inc. and digital marketing manager for AOL since September 2017. Not only that, the Sitemap pages for Sumeru Inc. and Sumeru Ventures indicated that they were modified right after The Morning Context story.

Take a moment and let it all sink in. Two people with absolutely no history of investment or managing capital become managing directors of a fund that doesn't have any clear source of funding and then go on announcing investments worth hundreds of millions of dollars in sundry unicorns, including Byju's.

It took about two weeks to comb through the internet and dozens of phone calls to gather all the information. Then we joined the dots and The Morning Context broke the story of the phantom fundraising.

A few hours after the story was published on 4 July, I received a call from Raveendran. His explanation: he was a victim. He told me that there were no reasons for him to doubt the intentions of Sumeru Ventures since an existing investor referred them. Raveendran also said that there was no way for him or his team to find out Sumeru Ventures' antecedents.

This, I told him, was unconvincing. No one does multi-million dollar deals without doing proper due diligence about the individuals or the companies involved. But he stuck to his explanation and I, to my conclusion. By the end of the day, as we expected, the news of the phantom fundraising spread like, wildfire and every publication picked up the story.

———

It has become a pattern over the last year. Every time I write about Byju's, Raveendran and I end up talking at great length. Most times, these conversations are rhetorical and lead nowhere. And yes, he always asks what I personally, or The Morning Context as an organization, have against him.

The truth is people talk, or gossip if you prefer the term, about things that grow too big – governments, children, companies or lies. Journalists who cover beats and companies know this. People start giving them tips and trusting them with information. Somebody sneaks into Twitter (X) DM, or drops a message on IM. The more careful informants create anonymous email accounts.

A few days after The Morning Context published the story about Sumeru Ventures' investment that wasn't there, we got another tip. We learnt that it wasn't the first time Byju's had announced an investment that didn't come through.

We learnt money from Oxshott Capital Partners, or related entities, for an investment announced in September 2021, hadn't come through either. The venture capital firm was supposed to lead a ₹2,200 crore investment with the investment of ₹1,200 crore. In turn, this was to be part of a larger Series F round that valued Byju's at $18 billion.

Try a Google search (or use Bing or Yahoo or any other search engine) for Oxshott Venture Fund X LLC and you will find no results before or after the announcement of the investment in Byju's. This limited liability company was incorporated in Delaware, US, on 14 September 2021, less than two weeks before Byju's shareholders passed a resolution for the said fundraising.

There are no details about who is running the fund. Not even an email address is visible. So, I downloaded the incorporation documents from Delaware's Department of State website. These documents list Legalinc Corporate Services as the fund's registered agent. There is no other detail whatsoever.

I reached out to Legalinc several times. First via email. There was no reply. I followed up with another email the next day. No reply this time either. So, I called up the phone number for Legalinc listed on the Delaware Department of State's website. The call went to the board and was directed to customer care. Over the call, the executive said that 'unfortunately, we can't give out any information that is not public knowledge'.

That was strike one.

I decided to look up other variations of Oxshott Venture Fund and found an Oxshott Venture Fund IX LLC on the

US Securities and Exchange Commission website. This fund was also incorporated in Delaware in 2021. The SEC filing names Erne Stern as the manager of Oxshott Venture Fund IX LLC. I called the number mentioned in the SEC filing. It went straight to voicemail. Several attempts thereafter to reach the number went in vain.

Next, I did a Google search for the phone number. It returned a name. It was a real estate agent with the same last name at Keller Williams Valley Realty in Woodcliff Lake, New Jersey, which, coincidentally, also employs Erne Stern's wife. I also wrote to Stern on LinkedIn, but again, there was no response.

Strike two.

Stern, I discovered, is the managing director at Oxshott Capital Partners LLC, an independent boutique investment banking and advisory firm. The firm's website is as good as non-existent. All it has is an address, an email and the name of the company it offers securities through. I sent an email to the address listed on the website, but it did not get delivered. I also found an email address that seemed to belong to Stern and shot him an email, which also bounced back. I wrote to Oxshott Capital Partners CEO Kara Boyle, but again received no reply.

Another dead end. Strike three.

Here was another company no one knew anything about. It was a deja vu moment for me. This, increasingly, looked like another phantom investor.

But Byju's kept hoping the money would come. In subsequent board resolutions passed through March 2022, the name of Oxshott or its related entities kept featuring. The money never came, though.

In his usual off-the-record calls before the story was published, Raveendran told me the VC firm belonged to a very respectable family office in the US. One or some investors to the fund were from Russia and the money hadn't come through because of the ongoing Russia–Ukraine war.

A convenient answer? Or an unfortunate coincidence? Make what you want of it but the fact remains that the money never reached the Byju's accounts. And as expected, this news break was also picked up by multiple Indian and international publications.

Raveendran has since accepted in interviews with publications that two investments – Sumeru and Oxshott – never came through. On one occasion, in an interview with the financial portal Moneycontrol, he said, 'Now, the $300 million from Sumeru and Oxshott is not coming, but that is not our mistake. But who cares about $300 million? I can raise $300 million in a week.'

What happened in these two cases was not very common but such things do happen. Start-ups raise funds that keep bumping up their valuations. Sometimes, these funds don't come in. No one checks and the company doesn't have a legal obligation to inform anybody. A listed company in Byju's place, for example, would have to inform the stock exchanges as well as the capital market regulator, SEBI or the SEC, as the case might be. But a private company only has to file the relevant information with the Registrar of Companies.

But these two phantom investments do give rise to one very important question: why was the Byju's board silent when this happened?

A finance professional who has worked with many listed and unlisted companies told me that this is all about greed and fear. When things are going well, it is about greed. And when they turn bad, it is the fear of losing everything, so everyone stays silent.

It is hard to believe that Raveendran was fooled twice: first with Oxshott and then with Sumeru. As they say, fool me once, shame on you; fool me twice, shame on me. But the alternate explanations lead into legally dubious territory.

Why would a company conceal the fact that an investment had not occurred, not once but twice?

I will leave that question hanging but here is a fact for readers to ponder. The company's valuation rose from $18 billion in September 2021 to $22 billion in March 2022. This came on the back of funding announcements, which actually had a gaping hole of ₹2,500 crore in terms of investments that did not actually materialize.

9

The Turning Point

'Not all media.'

The senior vice president, communications, at Byju's sent this reply to my WhatsApp text on 13 September 2022. Earlier that day, I learnt that the company was reaching out to journalists for a 20-minute briefing the next day. There was a strong rumour that the company might release its earnings report for FY21 – the 12-month period that had ended on 31 March 2021 – at the briefing.

Technically, private companies have to file their financials with India's Ministry of Corporate Affairs by September of the next fiscal year – that is within six months. But delays in filing have become the norm over the years. Byju's has a particularly terrible record when it comes to this. Its audited earnings report for FY20 was filed with an 18-month delay in September 2021. It was September again and there was no news on the FY21 numbers yet. Speculations were rife. So, when the news about the press briefing came in, there was a lot of interest.

Naturally, we at The Morning Context were surprised (okay, that was mostly me) to not have any information about the event. So I sent text messages over WhatsApp to both Raveendran and the communications head.

'Hear you guys are offering 20 min briefings tomorrow to all media people. I still don't have it,' I wrote. Pat came the reply mentioned above. So, I wrote back: 'Noted. Thanks.'

Then came another message: 'If we create slots in the following day, will share.'

Raveendran replied after a few hours: 'Happy to meet whenever you have time for a long meeting (not just 20 mins). As you can see on top, I have been requesting both of you for many weeks.'

He meant, Ashish, my editor, and I.

The next day, as was expected, the company released selected numbers to select journalists. The earnings report started getting circulated in no time. We managed to get hold of a copy too. It was 3.30 p.m. on 14 September.

For the next few hours, Ashish and I poured over the document. The numbers, as expected, were disastrous, but the document made for an interesting read. Here are the highlights:

- At a consolidated level, that's Byju's and WhiteHat Jr put together, revenue from operations had stagnated at ₹2,280 crore, compared with an adjusted revenue of ₹2,189 crore in 2019–20.
- Revenues came from the following sources:
    i)   Course fees: ₹320 crore
    ii) Streaming services: ₹108 crore
    iii) Sale of SD cards: ₹1,848 crore

The point to note here is that over 80% of Byju's operating revenue came from the sales of SD cards. For a company in the business of providing education, this is absurd. Once the card is shipped to the buyer, there is no way to prove it is being accessed and no way to judge if the Byju's app is actually helping children to learn anything. Indeed, many parents have complained that the tablet becomes a toy after a while.

- Losses jumped to ₹4,588 crore FY21, compared with losses ₹231 crore in the year before. Losses amounted to literally twice the revenues. The company actually filed a different set of numbers with the MCA. Those numbers showed substantial differences with the details shared with the media. The table below uses the MCA numbers.

These were terrible numbers, no matter how you looked at them. They were even worse if you consider two things: the revenue was flat and losses soared to record levels in a pandemic year, when the edtech business witnessed its biggest boom. In contrast, the revenue for rivals Unacademy and Vedantu, for example, rose 6x and 3x, respectively, in the same period.

Also, Raveendran had been claiming through 2020–21 that the company was doubling its top line and would record more than ₹5,000 crore in revenue. That didn't happen. Byju's lost around ₹12.5 crore daily in FY21.

Byju's Rising Losses

Fiscal Period	Revenues (₹ Cr)	Net Loss (₹ Cr)
2020–21	2,428.4	-4,564.4
2019–20	2,511.8	-305.5
2018–19	1,366.9	-8.8
2017–18	500.2	-37.2

The other standout detail from the earnings report was that Deloitte, Byju's auditor, finally ran out of patience with the company's fuzzy accounting practices and put its foot down. It remains a mystery why one of the world's biggest accounting firms took so long to identify and address such a massive issue, something that journalists had been talking about for months.

Byju's sells multi-year courses bundled with a tablet and an SD card. This has been their main business over the years. Now, about 9 out of 10 sales are three- to five-year plans. So, the company should ideally recognize only a part of the income accrued from the sale in the financial year in which the sale is made. But Byju's position is that once the SD card is delivered to the customer and the money is collected in full, the transaction is complete. So, it shows the entire revenue collected for several years as the revenue for the year of sale.

For years, Raveendran claimed his product was like an iPhone. Apple sells an iPhone and books the entire amount as revenue for the year of the sale, because it considers the transaction complete and Byju's felt it could do the same.

This is flawed logic in accounting terms. For starters, Apple, or any such company that sells products doesn't have a multi-year contract for the product with the customer. It may charge annual fees later for repair and maintenance beyond the warranty period, but the product itself is sold in a one-time transaction. The transaction is really over as soon as the sale is made.

Education, however, is a multi-year service. In Byju's case, for example, the company charges for the tablet and SD card as well as the multi-year course on it. So, the company is responsible for the customer for the duration of the course.

Second, this method of revenue recognition doesn't take into account returns which, according to many people in the industry – both inside the company and outside – are in the range of 20%. If a customer cancels a course, the company has to either refund the money, or part of the money. It should mark returns as a separate line entry or clearly indicate if the revenue it is recognizing on the topline is adjusted for returns.

The problem becomes even more complex when you consider that a majority of Byju's customers take loans to buy the courses. So, while the company books the revenue for multiple years at the time of sale, the customer continues paying the lender for years.

This has several implications. If the customer stops paying, Byju's and the loan provider would share the losses according to the terms of the FLDG. But then retrospective changes to the accounts may be necessary if, for example, the customer stops paying in year two of a five-year course and the entire five years of revenue has been recognized as received in year one.

Essentially, such a practice of recognizing all revenues upfront neglects the possibility of defaults and makes it hard to judge the level of returns. It also makes it impossible for an investor to judge the tenure of the courses.

If you're an investor who's considering investing in an edtech business, you will want to know a lot of details that aren't available because the Byju's accounts aren't transparent. For example, you may want to know the following:

- How many customers sign up for three years, or five years or other tenure?
- What are the levels of returns and the quantum of refunds?
- Is the revenue adjusted for these refunds or do the accounts merely show refunds as bundled expenses or some other opaque charge?
- How many courses are funded on EMI?
- What are the typical FLDGs exposures and the credit costs of such funding?

In a transparent set of accounts, where revenue recognition is done conventionally, these details would be clearly and transparently available. Ideally these details would perhaps be laid out in a separate KPI (key performance indicator) document attached to the Profit and Loss account.

In the audited earnings report for FY21, Deloitte put an end to this practice of revenue recognition upfront. It had been going on for years. The most significant change in Byju's audited earnings report for FY21 is, therefore, how the company recognizes revenues.

Here's what Deloitte has to say on the subject:

Revenues from transfer of products to certain customers made under deferred payment terms and totalling to Rs 1,156.27 crore (based on consideration that the Parent is entitled for such transfers) has not been recognised because on the point of these transfers the Parent did not meet the criteria that it was probable it will collect the consideration to which it is entitled.

Long story short – the auditor insisted that more than ₹1,150 crore that the company would have claimed as revenues under its earlier accounting practices, should be lopped off. Some or all of this revenue may actually be recognized in later years.

This is also testimony to the fact that Byju's sales team excels in one-time sales. Salespeople never bother to check whether the customers actually pay up the full amount over the duration of the course. It is one reason why the company focus has always been on making more sales rather than following up with existing customers on services quality and taking their feedback. The company prefers to book revenue in the year of sale. The salespeople are expected to move on and find new customers to show growth.

There is more from Deloitte:

In the current year, the Parent has retrospectively adjusted the following: A. Revenues from streaming services, which was previously recognised fully on commencement of contract, has been adjusted to be recognised rateably over the period of the contract. B. Interest paid to loan partners on behalf of customers in respect of loans granted directly to customers have been reclassified from finance cost and adjusted against revenues, since these payments are in the nature of payments to customers.

'A' indicates the auditor has made what adjustments it could retrospectively to align revenue recognition standards, which means prior years' accounts will have changed significantly. 'B' indicates that it has tried to adjust credit costs against revenues, which imparts more transparency.

There's more to come in the way of auditor's notes. But in order to understand the business, it is important to put things in context. If you have a finance or accounting background and wish to understand the details, read through the following extract from the notes to accounts. Otherwise, you can skip the next section and just read the explanation.

The following extract from the notes to accounts shows how the auditor has tried to clarify revenue recognition. If it's the sale of an SD card, the revenue can be recognized upfront, but if it's a multi-year course, the revenue will be recognized over the tenure of the course.

Moreover, potential exposure to Byju's under the FLDG terms with its lenders should also be assessed at fair value and netted off against revenues. This will be a moving target – as each EMI payment comes in, the FLDG exposure drops.

(i)   . . . Revenue is recognised upon transfer of control of promised products or services to customers in an amount that reflects the consideration the Group expects to receive in exchange for those products or services. To recognise revenues, the Group applies the following five-step approach:

(1) identify the contract with a customer,

(2) identify the performance obligations in the contract,

(3) determine the transaction price,

(4) allocate the transaction price to the performance obligations in the contract, and

(5) recognise revenues when a performance obligation is satisfied. When there is uncertainty as to collectability, revenue recognition is deferred to a point in time when substantially all of the promised consideration has been collected from the customer and the consideration is non refundable.

(ii) The group in its normal course of business sells educational content to its customers via SD cards (categorised as Sale of Edutech products) and provides the content in the form of Streaming services (categorised as Sale of services). In the case of Sale of content via SD cards, the Group does not have any continuing performance obligations once the content filled SD cards are made available to the customers. The Sale of Edutech products (which includes sale of tablets) are recognised at a point in time. In the case of sale of educational content in the form of Streaming services, revenue is recognised over the period of time the services are rendered to the customers.

(iii) Sale of Edutech products to customers primarily involves 3 modes of settlement by customers:

(a) where the customer pays all the consideration upfront.

(b) where the customer chooses to take a loan from a Loan partner (refer note (iv) below)

(c) where the Parent provides extended credit terms (refer (v) below).

(iv) In cases where the customer takes a loan from the Loan partners, the customer makes a down payment to the Parent and the balance consideration is settled by the Loan partner. The Parent receives the balance consideration from the Loan partner net of subvention costs charged by the Loan partner to the Parent. The subvention costs being in the nature of interest paid on behalf of customers are netted off against revenue.

Under the aforesaid arrangements with Loan partners, the Parent has provided guarantees (First Loss Default Guarantees (FLDG) to the Loan partners and is obligated to reimburse the Loan partners for any monthly instalments that remain uncollected by the Loan partner and stay overdue for a prescribed period (which typically ranges between 'overdue for 75 days or 90 days' across the arrangements with the Loan partners). The Parent estimates fair value of the aforesaid guarantee obligations and accrues for the same.

The difference between the consideration received by the Parent from the (i) customer and the Loan partner and (ii) the fair value of the guarantee at the time of entering into the contract with the customer is recognised as revenue. The estimates of the fair value of guarantee are revisited at the end of every period closing and any changes in the fair value are accounted for as a change in the estimates.

(v) In cases where the customers are provided deferred payment terms by the Parent the customers are required to pay a part of the consideration ('down payment'), at the time the customers buys the product/ services and the customers are also required to register an e-NACH mandate in favour of the Parent. Post payment of the down payment, the customer pays the balance consideration over the contract period (in monthly instalments which typically range from 3 months to 12 months). In such cases, the Parent determines whether the terms of sale indicate the existence of a contract under the provisions of Ind AS 115 – Revenue from Contracts with Customers, with particular reference to whether there is a probability of collection of the consideration.

The earnings report, as well as Deloitte's detailed notes, especially on revenue recognition, make it clear that the revenue growth story the company had been weaving together over the years was misleading and opaque at best, and at worst it was perhaps made out of thin air, given the horrific spike in losses. While the company may claim all this to be mere accounting details, it certainly isn't trivial.

Bluntly, Deloitte is saying that Byju's revenue numbers were exaggerated.

What the company was calling revenue, was actually the 'booking value'. Think of it as the gross merchandise value in e-commerce, which is the total value of goods sold, without accounting for discounts and returns. Actual revenue figures in the case of Byju's, like in the case of e-commerce businesses, would be the booking numbers minus cancellations and returns. And yes, you will have to divide the revenue by the number of years the courses have been taken for.

But it is the booking value that gets the full attention and hence is a pivotal number. This is the number around which the business revolves and on which targets and incentives depend. Byju's ability to raise funds, and by extension its valuation, depended less on its earnings report from the previous year, and more on the booking numbers from the last few months.

There were other glaring issues visible in the FY21 earnings report. For example, there was a massive 60% drop in the India business. This was unbelievable, considering this was the pandemic year.

Apart from the changes in revenue recognition norms, one thing could explain this: fake sales. Salespeople, under immense pressure to achieve targets, would ask friends and family members to book courses and then cancel within a few days.

Salespeople, as I wrote in a previous chapter, sometimes put in more than ₹15,000 as a down payment from their own pocket to punch in a sale of, say, ₹2.5 lakh. They make the booking, clock in the revenue, and then cancel the subscription in a few days and claim the refund. Simple. Effective. There are many other ways to make fake sales.

It is not that this practice was unknown. Showing inflated bookings is an open secret and mostly an accepted sin in the edtech world. In many conversations, industry executives as well as edtech experts have pointed this out to me. But the audited FY21 report made it official and a matter of public record, one that can't be disputed any more. The scale of the problem obviously runs into hundreds or even thousands of crores.

This earnings report would destroy the company's dreams. Not only did it dash all hopes for a possible IPO in the near future, it changed the outlook of the entire sector and led to pointed questions about inflated valuations and the diagnosis of an edtech bubble.

It became even more difficult for edtech companies to raise capital, which triggered massive cost-cutting exercises across the edtech spectrum as companies became desperate to conserve cash and increase their runway. There's another very interesting aspect of the 2020–21 earnings, which seems to have so far escaped the scrutiny it deserves. We called it the Djinn of the desert when we came across it. This made Byju's earnings more palatable but doesn't seem to have a solid foundation.

One of the silver linings in the 2020–21 earnings report is the company's revenues from the Middle East, which doubled to ₹497 crore from ₹244 crore in the previous financial year. Remember, during this period, the revenue from India declined to ₹987 crore from ₹1,603 crore. This meant that revenue from the Gulf Cooperation Council countries was almost 50% of Byju's India revenue and it was consistently rising. Here's the note from Deloitte on revenue from the Middle East:

Revenues from sale of educational content to customers based in the Gulf Cooperation Council (GCC) countries amounts to Rs. 497 Crores (Rs. 245 Crores in the year ended March 31,2020). All sales of the Parent to these customers are invoiced on an unrelated entity located out of Dubai (refer note 2.4a(ii)). The Parent pays the aforesaid entity a commission on such sales. Commission paid/payable during the year Rs. 237 Crores (Previous year ended March 31, 2020 Rs. 115.01 crores) have been disclosed under Commission expenses in the Statement of Profit and Loss.

Unlike in India or the US, where Byju's either provides the product and services itself, or owns the subsidiary that does so, the structure in the Middle East is different. Byju's operations in the region are handled by More Ideas General Trading Llc (MIGT), a Dubai-based company that operates in the United Arab Emirates, Oman, Kuwait, Qatar and Saudi Arabia.

Not much is known about the company or its structure. Its social media pages are practically non-existent. According to its Facebook profile, it used to be a distributor of tablets at one time. Now, it calls itself the Middle East office of Byju's.

The company works as an unrelated commission agent that identifies customers and does last-mile deliveries for a fee. Byju's invoices all its sales to MIGT and books the revenue. Here's what Deloitte has to say about Byju's sales arrangement in the Middle East:

(ii) Sale to retail customers in the Gulf Cooperation Council (GCC) countries

In respect of sales to retail customers in the Gulf Cooperation Council (GCC) countries, the Parent invoices all its sales to an unrelated entity ('Counter party') located in Dubai and also pays the Counter party sales commission. Judgement is required to determine whether the Counter party is an agent. Under the arrangement with the Counter party:

- the Parent provides educational content only after a retail customer is identified by the Counter party.
- the Counter party does not have a right to redirect the Group's products to any other customers without getting instructions from the Parent.
- the Parent continues to be responsible to compensate the end customer in cases of product returns.

The Parent has concluded that the Counter party is an agent and accordingly records the commission expense and the sales on a gross basis. Refer note 24(ii).

An arrangement like this, though complex, is perfectly acceptable legally. But there are several intriguing details. The first is the ₹497 crore revenue. The total population of the GCC countries in 2020 was 57.7 million, with just under 9 million schoolgoing children. India, in comparison, had around 250 million schoolgoing children. This makes the GCC revenue numbers seem rather too good to be true.

Industry watchers have always been sceptical about the Middle East revenues. A former employee who knew the systems well told me that these sales were not punched into the Indian transaction system as invoices were raised directly. Consequently, there had always been concerns about the veracity of revenues from the Middle East.

Another edtech watcher who knows the company's Middle East operations told me the numbers were ridiculous. 'The Middle East business is a very small business. It is so small that the guy running it had to sometimes send visas and call salespeople from India,' he told me.

The best year, said this person, was 2017–18 when the company did business in low double-digit crores. That was when Think & Learn, Byju's parent company, organized a quiz contest in association with the Asianet television channel.

'During Covid, this business was completely broken. So, I am as surprised as you to see the huge revenue figures,' he said.

There is also the question of how Byju's is recording returns. The earnings report doesn't have anything on the number of returns. But assuming returns at 20% – in line with the India business – Byju's would have to pay MIGT around ₹100 crore for the returned products. It is not clear whether the ₹497 crore revenue is before or after adjusting for returns.

We asked Byju's about the Middle East business. Here's what the company said in its response:

As a group that spans many countries around the world, BYJU'S has multiple partnerships with local companies for distributing our content and products. The exact nature of the partnership depends on the specific requirements and laws and the regions BYJU'S serves, including MENA (Middle East and North Africa) to which you have referred. All applicable tax laws in India and around the world are adhered to in both letter and spirit.

That response amounts to a long-winded way to say nothing. Then there is also the question of taxes on the ₹237 crore commission paid to MIGT. The earnings report doesn't have details on this either. This is a huge grey area in which companies love to operate. Byju's, for example, filed an application before the Authority for Advance Ruling, Mumbai, in 2019, saying that the payment made to MIGT, a non-resident entity, was not chargeable to tax and, therefore, it was not required to deduct tax at source. As things stand, we don't know how much tax Byju's has paid on commissions given to MIGT, or the revenues it has booked from the Middle East business. We also don't have any information on the tax liability of these two heads.

Finally, there are questions about delivery, product efficacy and learning outcomes. No one knows if the products sold to MIGT reached the students. The number of products unsold or returned can't be ascertained without an audit of MIGT. If it were a subsidiary, the accounts would have been consolidated and things would have been clearer. But since it is not, you could claim any number and it would fly.

———

In his post-earnings interview with Moneycontrol, you can see Raveendran at his charming best. There is a certain air of nonchalance about his demeanour as he rubbishes all the concerns and paints a rosier and larger-than-life picture of the company and its prospects. So far so good. Any good entrepreneur would do the same; focus on the future and try to make it look better than the past, even in the middle of a crisis. But there is a thin line between making hopeful projections, giving selective information and lying. There is one sentence in the interview that caught a lot of people, including me, off guard. If memory serves me well, at least five people sent a screenshot of that sentence to me.

Asked whether there was a cash crunch at the company, given that the investments from Sumeru Ventures and Oxshott Capital had not materialized and the company hadn't yet paid up for the acquisition of Aakash, Raveendran rubbished the concerns, saying, 'It's a joke when people say that we are running out of cash.' Then he continued, 'Now, the $300 million from Sumeru and Oxshott is not coming, but that is not our mistake. But who cares about $300 million? I can raise $300 million in a week.'

As they say in the porn industry, that statement was the money shot! I wasn't the only person who thought the last statement was cocky and arrogant. Confidence is one thing. Taking your investors for granted is completely different. This statement suggested the latter.

As things turned out, Raveendran has since not been able to raise fresh capital in any of the companies of the group. There was a $250 million investment from Qatar Investment Authority in October 2022, which, it seems, he used to pay for the acquisition of Aakash. But it was not primary or fresh capital entirely. Negotiations for this must have started long before the earnings announcements. There was also a debt-raising round of around $250 million from American investment fund Davidson Kempner in May 2023, which also came in against the assumed future cash flows in Aakash.

Since the Moneycontrol interview, there have been many announcements of billion-dollar capital infusions, but all Byju's has been able to raise so far has been the money from QIA and the debt from Davidson Kempner. That 'I can raise $300 million in a week' statement has become an albatross around his neck. The two stories we broke on the phantom fundraises were where the spiral began. The earnings announcement was the cold confirmation that the finances were in terrible shape.

The FY21 report also triggered a series of events. First, as I said before, funding dried. One edtech executive told me there were too many red flags in the FY21 earning reports, which spooked the investors. 'Talking about raising $300 million in a week is easy. Going out in the market with an earnings report like this and raising funds is the difficult part,' he told me. The truth is that public bravado apart, the top management was becoming acutely aware of the crisis at hand.

In the second week of October, Gokulnath and Mohit issued separate statements, suggesting the company would lay off 2,500 employees in six months. The layoffs, they said, were to reduce redundancies as the company consolidated its subsidiaries into one India business and started focusing on sustainable growth and profitability.

In her statement, Gokulnath said the jobs cuts would happen across 'product, content, media, and technology teams in a phased manner' over the next six months, without divulging details. At the time, the company claimed it employed over 50,000 people. While the statements from her or Mohit didn't mention layoffs in the sales team, the biggest churn was apparently happening in that group itself. According to several current and former Byju's salespeople at the time, 500 sales executives were fired in Bengaluru alone. One person told me that the company was finding excuses to sack salespersons.

There was something odd about the manner in which the layoffs were announced. It wasn't like this was the first mass layoff at Byju's. But never before had the company proactively made such an announcement beforehand. It surprised even those who knew the company and its founders well. Byju's was trying to make the landing softer. But for what? We guessed it could only be one thing. But all we had at the moment was a theory. We had no confirmations.

In its response to our queries about the layoffs, the company said 'not more than 2,500 jobs will be cut as part of the ongoing resource rationalization drive . . . BYJU'S takes its role as India's largest job creator among start-ups seriously. At this point, ceteris paribus, the company anticipates no more rationalization drive. The churn from the sales team – and the ongoing pan-India sales hiring drive – is a part of the business-as-usual scenario,' the company said in its response. 'Please note that BYJU'S has more than 10,000 sales staff and managers on its payroll across India. This rationalization also extends to our marketing efforts. As mentioned before, BYJU'S is moving towards an inside sale-driven model where the ease of scaling up the team and customer satisfaction are higher, while the cost of sales is far lower than field sales. As a global company, BYJU'S branding efforts will now focus as much on the rest of the world as it would on India.'

Two things were worth noting in the statement. One, Byju's was moving away from field sales, the force behind its unbridled growth over the years. Two, in the garb of increasing customer satisfaction and lowering costs, the company was accepting that customers were not completely satisfied with the model of aggressive field sales.

Naturally, when you move to sales over video conferencing from field sales, a lot of jobs would become redundant. So, we kept digging about the real number of layoffs. Unsurprisingly, it was way more than the company announced.

———

10 p.m., Wednesday, 26 October 2022.

I got a call from Raveendran. We were writing a story for the next morning, saying Byju's was laying off close to 25% of its workforce – around 12,000 people.

> **Raveendran:** I can prove this number is wrong. At the end of the month, I can show you the salary slips and I can show you the salary slips of the last month. So, whoever is feeding you [the information], you have to do something about it. This is not a joke.
>
> **Me:** This is not one person. There are multiple people from different circles.
>
> **BR:** I am telling you I will show you the proof of money transferred. You can see the number yourself. I will show you September-end, October-end and November-end also. There has to be some responsibility, Pradip. Whoever is feeding you the information is giving you the wrong information. We will file a case against them.

Me: But they are not saying these many people are already fired. They are saying this is the plan.

BR: How can they? Without me knowing, there can't be a plan of [laying off] 15,000 people. I am telling you; I will show you not just past but also future . . . You can see monthly payouts and see how many people we are paying and you can see whether the numbers are going down by 2,500 or 15,000.

Someone who is angry with us is feeding you wrong info. I am not saying they don't have a reason to be angry. But the information is wrong. And they have fed this information to others as well.

. . .

If you continue writing like this, I will be forced to fire all 15,000 people. Do you want to be responsible for that by writing this much fake news?

Me: Hmm.

. . .

BR: You are not checking for veracity, Pradip. Will this person be accountable if we take this to court? These are random anonymous people. This is not happening. This, I am sure someone is giving the same info to multiple people . . .

What proof he has? Is he the HR head? If outside partners are doing this, we have no control over it. But we can't do this, no? If employees take us to court, what can we do? There is a contract. We don't have plans to lay off even 5,000 people.

Me: I trust my sources. They were right about the SPAC issue. They were right about Sumeru and Oxshott . . .

BR: But I never said I got money from Sumeru . . .

Me: I never said you said that. I am just saying I trust my sources on this because they have been correct in the past.

BR: This is wrong and if you write like this, you will create panic and you will ensure that thousands of families are losing jobs by creating panic.

Me: Hmm.

This call went on for close to 20 minutes with no real answers.

I had multiple confirmations that the company was firing between 12,000 and 15,000 people from various departments, including sales and corporate functions, with the sales team being the worst hit. Managers were left without an answer when sacked people questioned, 'Why was my job terminated?' The situation, I was told, was the worst in Bengaluru, especially at the IBC Knowledge Park office. The business model in itself had become an issue. The pressure of cutting costs was immense.

At Byju's offices, especially in Bengaluru, there was chaos, confusion and denial. Things were so bad that if a person was not seen in the office for even one day, they would receive calls from colleagues asking if/why they had been sacked. Everyone was asking, 'Why me?' No one had the answer.

Many employees had been asked to resign with short notice periods. Salespeople who were not able to meet at least 50% of their monthly targets were being asked to leave immediately. Several of the employees who had been asked to leave were not even offered a proper settlement.

The sector isn't new to layoffs. Since schools had started reopening, thousands of employees in edtech companies had lost their jobs. It was symptomatic of an industry shrinking as rapidly as it had expanded. Edtech companies hired indiscriminately during the pandemic years when the cost of capital was cheaper, the market was flush with liquidity and growth was the only target. But liquidity dried up and the edtech industry had been caught off guard. Growth plans fizzled out.

But even keeping all this in mind, the numbers at Byju's were mind-boggling, both in absolute terms and as a percentage of the company's workforce. It was also a sign that Raveendran had finally acknowledged the cost structure was unsustainable. The company had decided to focus entirely on reducing expenses by whatever means necessary. Raveendran also realized that the sales practices were at the heart of the problem, and needed to be fixed if the company was to be saved.

Byju's is a sales machine on steroids and the salespeople are the lifeblood of the machine. It is the salespeople who bring most, if not all, of the company's revenues. Naturally, the sales team is one of the largest and most overworked. Over the years, it had also grown exponentially because of Byju's dependence on direct sales.

But the company had put on a lot of flab in the pandemic years to the extent that one team was cannibalizing another team's sales. Job cuts, therefore, were inevitable. The situation worsened because the fundraising was not going as per plan.

So, neither the fact of the layoffs nor their scale was surprising. While the company did PR around 2,500 layoffs, the real numbers were a multiple of that. We published the story the next morning.

———

At 9.14 a.m. on Thursday, 27 October 2022, I got a text message from Raveendran on WhatsApp.

'Please don't create panic among employees. We are not letting go of 12k people. Why are you doing this?'

Then a missed call at 9.15 a.m. I was in the middle of making breakfast.

A few minutes later, we were on a call.

BR: This is unfair, Pradip. You are creating panic among our employees. Who is giving you the information?

Me: But employees are already in a panic, given the layoffs.

. . .

BR: You writing this, this is affecting employees. I am asking you, not as a journalist, but as a human being, you don't care about these many employees? Do you actually care or you don't care, my question is that. If you care, today what you have done, has created so much panic . . . Now all 50,000 [employees] are panicking . . . Can you ask for proof, how is this 15,000 or 12,000, whatever. Does this person have a list?

Me: I don't know if he has . . .

BR: When you write this, there is so much panic. When you say 12,000, all the 50,000 will panic. That's not the plan . . .

Now, because of this, if we are forced to fire so many people, will you take responsibility for that?

Me: Please don't pin it on me. I wasn't the one who hired those people. I didn't change business models. I didn't fire them. I wasn't responsible for your growth two years back and I am not responsible now . . .

The call went on for about 10 minutes, but we kept going around the issue in circles. Raveendran kept telling me how I was helping people who wanted to spread misinformation and I kept insisting on how I believed my sources.

At 10.37 a.m., Raveendran sent me a screenshot of the string of messages the company posted on Twitter (X).

In those, Byju's categorically denied that the job cuts were more than 2,500. But then this wasn't the first time the company was lying. Data from the EPFO would prove that.

According to EPFO data, accessed by PrivateCircle Research, the number of employees at Byju's – and I am only talking about the parent company – declined to 37,509 in November 2022 from 48,143 in September. The Employee count peaked at 58,000-plus in March 2022, and it was down to less than 25,000 by June 2023.

Employee Count at Byju's

Date	Employees
Mar 2020	13,764
Mar 2021	29,164
Mar 2022	58,292
Mar 2023	27,341
Jun 2023	24,659

Source: PrivateCircle Research

Raveendran was right in that he had never said that he had raised money from Sumeru Ventures and Oxshott Capital. But his company had announced fundraises that included capital from these two funds. It received a higher valuation in subsequent rounds on the assumption that all the money had landed in its accounts. But the company never clarified that the capital from Sumeru Ventures and Oxshott Capital never hit its accounts. The admission that those investments had not arrived and might never come was not made until The Morning Context published these stories and people started asking questions.

———

While all this was happening – the company was facing a severe cash crunch and was firing people en masse – we also learnt that the promoters – founder Byju Raveendran, his brother Riju Ravindran and Byju's wife, Divya Gokulnath – had sold 25% of their total holdings between 2016 and 2021, according to documents accessed from the website of India's Ministry of Corporate Affairs. In those five years, the company's valuation rose by 28x.

At that time, we didn't have complete data on how many shares were sold by whom and when, but our conservative estimate and back-of-the-envelope calculations suggested that the promoters would have made anywhere around $100–$250 million through this secondary sale of shares in Byju's.

A secondary sale of shares in a private company is when a founder sells their shares to an existing investor or a third party to make money. These transactions are usually done with the blessing of investors in the company. In itself, a secondary sale of shares is not an unusual event; founders and early investors do it all the time.

The case of Byju's promoters cashing out is important purely because of the amount of personal wealth the founders have accumulated. The quantum of sales also leads one to believe that they didn't trust the valuations themselves – after all, if you think you own a chunk of a good, fast-growth business, why would you sell such a large stake?

PrivateCircle Research pulled out the data in July 2023 and according to their research, the promoters sold shares worth around $408.53 million in 40 secondary transactions since 2015.

These secondary deals were often executed at a discounted valuation to the company's primary valuation at the time. For instance, an average of 53% discount was observed in secondary sales during its Series F round, according to PrivateCircle Research analysis. While the company issued primary shares in the range of ₹2.1–2.4 lakh in its Series F round, its promoters sold them at a price range of ₹1.12–1.64 lakh apiece during the same period.

Raveendran often talks about putting money back into the company. 'If you give me even ₹100, I will invest it back in Byju's,' he told me in one of our interactions. While this might be true, the data suggests it is not.

The magnitude of the secondary sales also raised an important question: How much stake should venture investors allow entrepreneurs to dilute through secondary transactions?

VC investors are generally okay with founders carrying out secondary sales for a multitude of reasons, but even the most generous investors are uncomfortable once the dilution is more than 10% of the founder's stake. A little dilution shows there is value in the company and it could be the entrepreneur is raising some cash for personal reasons. But too much dilution and you signal imminent value erosion. Or that you have checked out of the business through the back door after having made your fortune.

In Byju's, promoters have sold 25% of their equity, which is way out of the comfort zone for most investors. It's baffling that Riju Ravindran, for instance, offloaded such a large number of shares in a matter of months.

Around the same time in November 2022, Prosus, the Netherlands-listed international internet assets arm of South African group Naspers, said the fair value of its 9.67% stake in Byju's was $578 million. It would mean that the investment company believes the fair value of India's largest edtech firm was actually $5.97 billion.

This was 73% below the $22 billion valuation at which the company said it raised funds in October 2022. Prosus's judgement wasn't the last word on Byju's valuation. Different investors value private companies differently in their accounts and it is possible that another shareholder would value Byju's differently.

Suffice it to say that Prosus's action did not mean a markdown of the shares. It was more like a conservative method of valuation. But still, it was bad news for the company, which had already been at the centre of multiple crises by then. It was also the beginning of a consistent decline in the business model and of sentiment around the company. The winter was setting in.

10

The Trainwreck

By the time December 2022 came, Byju's had lost all momentum. We discovered that for the first time in its history, Byju's, India's largest edtech company with a much-touted valuation of $22 billion, hadn't paid several of its vendors for months. Some of the payments had been pending since March 2022 – that is, the last financial year.

In the eight months to October 2022, cumulative dues to vendors had crossed ₹90 crore. Byju's, for instance, owed Amazon Web Services more than ₹26 crore, including GST, for its services. It also owed over ₹20 crore each to the messaging platform Gupshup and the real-time engagement platform Agora. Google and Facebook had even suspended the company's accounts for a while. They were only reactivated after partial payments were made. This was unusual. Vendors are usually paid within 30–60 days. In exceptional cases, the payments would stretch to 90–120 days but not beyond that.

It went from bad to worse. We also learnt that the company, again for the first time in its history, hadn't filed

TDS returns for months. Individual tax statements showed that Byju's last deposited TDS for April 2022. This could mean only one of two things. Either the company had deposited TDS and not filed returns, or the company hadn't deposited TDS at all. This, also, was unusual and it is taken very seriously by the tax authorities.

TDS is collected by employers on behalf of the Indian government. Employers are mandated to deposit TDS with the income tax department within a stipulated time. Apart from depositing TDS, employers are also mandated to file quarterly TDS returns. If a company deducts TDS but fails to deposit it with the government, it has to pay interest on the late payment at a rate of 1.5% per month. Missing the deadline for filing the TDS returns invites a late filing fee of ₹200 per day of delay. In addition, there is a penalty that can range between ₹10,000 and ₹1 lakh.

Long story short, there are only two reasons why TDS won't reflect in individual tax statements: Either the company doesn't have funds and hasn't paid or there is a wrong PAN linked for the employee. But with existing employees, this really couldn't be the reason.

So, the only reasonable explanation was that the company was going through a cash crunch. This came at a time when Byju's was hosting top executives and select guests in Qatar for the FIFA World Cup, of which it was a sponsor. This wasn't just bad optics; it was a travesty. But wait, there was even more to come.

Around February 2023, we discovered that Byju's was paying EMIs on behalf of customers who had cancelled their subscriptions, sought a refund and stopped paying EMIs.

Ideally, the company should have closed these subscriptions and paid back the lenders as its FLDG agreements mandated. But it didn't have the funds to do that. Since it was delaying the EMI payments as well, the customers who had cancelled also received a black mark on their credit records, apart from threatening calls from the lenders.

———

The funds crunch couldn't have come at a worse time. Byju's was struggling with the $1.2 billion term loan B it had raised in November 2021 and it was engaged in what would turn out to be a long legal battle.

When Byju's raised the term loan B, it was one of the largest such loans globally. Edtech was still riding the late tailwinds of the pandemic, interest rates were low and the funding winter was still a couple of months away. The company was on a buying spree in the international markets and the loan was supposed to fund inorganic growth. But then the market took a turn for the worse.

Byju's had raised the term loan at LIBOR plus 550 basis points – one basis point is one-hundredth of a percentage point. LIBOR, or the London Interbank Offered Rate, was the benchmark at the time at which overseas interest rates were set and borrowings in hard currency were often linked to LIBOR.

At the time Byju's had raised the term loan, LIBOR had been around 0.2%, which meant Byju's would have to pay 5.7% if the LIBOR stayed steady. But in one year, LIBOR had increased to 9%, which pushed the interest rate for Byju's up to 14.5%, adding more than $100 million of extra liability in terms of interest payments.

(On 30 June 2023, LIBOR was replaced by the Secured Overnight Financing Rate, or SOFR, a benchmark that is based on the rates US financial institutions pay each other for overnight loans.) Then the company breached a covenant of the credit agreement for the term loan by not filing the FY22 audited earnings in good time. As a result, the company lost access to the loan facility. Negotiations started and then broke down. In May, lenders sued Byju's Alpha, a US-based step-down subsidiary of Think & Learn, Byju's parent company.

The Morning Context sourced a non-redacted copy of the lenders' lawsuit in a Delaware court from an online legal research platform. The document has important details and establishes a timeline of events. It mentions how many times the borrowers (i.e. various Byju's entities) had accepted an event of default, agreed to make amends and then done nothing. We went through it a few times and decided that it was important in the public interest to talk about the assertions made by the lenders.

It was not about just the loan anymore. The matter is still sub judice. But if the court rules in favour of the lenders as it may well do, it could have huge implications for Byju's and, by extension, India's entire edtech sector. At stake here are the futures of millions of students whose parents have paid for courses in the hopes of a better education and better life for their children.

When Byju's raised the $1.2 billion term loan B in the US in November 2021 through Byju's Alpha, interest rates were near zero, the Covid-19 pandemic was still in full force, and online was the only mode of learning.

Four entities – Byju's Alpha (the borrower), the guarantors (which included Think & Learn, Byju's Pte. and Great Learning), GLAS Trust (the administrative and collateral agent) and initial lender Morgan Stanley Senior Funding Inc. – entered into the credit agreement by which Byju's Alpha raised the term loan. The company agreed to repay the loan in 'quarterly instalments of 0.25% of the aggregate principal, with the remainder of the principal due, absent an acceleration, on the term loan's maturity date'.

The lawsuit says Article 5 of the credit agreement lists several covenants made by each guarantor. Three covenants are worth mentioning here. From the lawsuit:

> 43. Article 5 of the Credit Agreement enumerates the affirmative covenants made by each Guarantor to the lenders. Pursuant to Section 5.1(a), Think and Learn covenanted to provide GLAS with its audited consolidated financial statements … for each fiscal year upon the conclusion of its annual audit (the 'Audit Covenant').
>
> 44. Pursuant to Section 5.1(b), Think and Learn further covenanted to provide GLAS with its unaudited consolidated financial statements for each fiscal quarter and the then-elapsed portion of each fiscal year at the conclusion of each fiscal quarter, as well as comparative figures for both the corresponding elapsed portion of, and corresponding fiscal quarter in, the previous fiscal year (the 'Statements Covenant').

47. Furthermore, pursuant to Section 5.9(c) of the Credit Agreement, the Guarantors covenanted that another one of Ravindran's companies, Whitehat Education Technology Private Limited ('Whitehat'), would accede to the Credit Agreement as a Guarantor (the 'Whitehat Guarantor Covenant').

The apparent gobbledegook translated to the following commitments. Audited financial statements would be filed annually and unaudited statements filed every quarter alongside filings of prior statements to help in the comparison of financial trends in the business. Also, WhiteHat Jr would need to come in as a guarantor.

Lenders claim the audit and statement covenants are significant as they help them track the company's financial health and make informed decisions about their credit risk. These include enforcing a number of other rights under the credit agreement, such as the right to financial information, the 'Maintenance of Properties', the 'Use of Proceeds' and the 'Guarantee Maintenance Requirement' covenants.

Article 8 of the agreement lists the circumstances that constitute events of default. It also describes the applicable cure period for each specified event of default. If the guarantors to the loan don't comply with the three covenants and 'if such covenant non-compliance is unremedied for 45 days', it constitutes an event of default.

If a default happens, the lawsuit claims that GLAS, as directed by 'required lenders', 'may accelerate the term loan and cause all outstanding term loan balances (together with interest thereon) to be due and payable immediately'. The required lenders, in this case, refers to a group of lenders who account for more than 50% of the 'total outstanding Term Loans and unused Term Commitments'.

Lenders claim in their lawsuit that the borrower failed to comply with these three covenants. Each of these breaches, mentions the lawsuit, resulted in independent events of default, which, put together, hampers the lenders' ability to monitor the business. The company also failed to provide the lenders with the WhiteHat India guarantee, which caused another event of default.

The lenders claim in the lawsuit that after 'multiple events of default', they put Byju's and Byju's Alpha on notice but still tried to work out a solution. Their counsel first wrote a letter on 29 August 2022 to Raveendran and the Byju's board of directors, concerned about their lack of engagement. It mentioned the lenders' concern about the company's financial disclosures, repeated delays in delivering audited financials for 2020–21 and the failure to adhere to the terms of the credit agreement.

The lenders' counsel sent a follow-up letter on 6 September, demanding a written response by 5 p.m. Eastern Time on 8 September. Raveendran responded on 7 September, acknowledging the loan parties' 'obligation to adhere strictly to the terms of the credit agreement' and saying that he 'will be working promptly to address them'. Byju's sent some information, lenders were not satisfied, letters and calls followed, and alternative paths forward were discussed.

Then nothing further happened, according to the lawsuit.

As time passed by without any solution, the 'lack of urgency and foot-dragging' by the loan parties frustrated the lenders. The lenders and the company were still negotiating and made multiple amendments to the credit agreement till 12 January 2023. One of these was a forbearance agreement, which came into effect on 13 January. The forbearance agreement reiterated that the specified defaults could not be cured or remedied until any such default is waived by the required lenders in writing. Byju's acknowledged, agreed and stipulated that as of 6 January 2023, the guarantors owed lenders $1.191 billion in principal on the term loan, in addition to accrued and unpaid interest.

The lenders' group followed this with reminders of consequences if no resolution could be found within the forbearance period. The lawsuit mentions three such reminders. But the warnings went unheeded and the forbearance period expired on 10 February. The lenders claim they continued seeking engagement from Byju's Alpha and the loan guarantors for a constructive resolution to no avail. As a result, they say, they were left with no choice but to protect the collateral for their loans.

So, on 3 March, GLAS delivered the Specified Notice of Acceleration to the loan parties, which made the entire principal amount of the term loans outstanding, plus accrued and unpaid interest, and other premiums and fees due and payable immediately. This was a trigger event, according to the pledge agreement and security agreement. The lawsuit claims that the trigger event enabled GLAS to secure and take control of the collateral. Singapore-based Byju's Pte., a wholly owned subsidiary of Byju's, had pledged 100% of its outstanding equity interests in Byju's Alpha to GLAS. Due to the trigger event, the suit claims, the Singapore company's voting and other consensual rights became vested in GLAS.

Also on 3 March, lenders directed GLAS to issue a formal Notice of Events of Default and Acceleration, which made more than $1.25 billion immediately due and payable.

If you look at the timeline of events since the debt was raised, you'll realize that it is a clear case of a calculated bet gone awry. The lenders in the lawsuit say that while they were attracted to the investment opportunity, their relationship with Raveendran and other loan parties became strained over time. Raveendran refused to accept this exercise of remedies. His representatives then threatened to classify the lenders as disqualified lenders. Meanwhile, he also approached lenders to negotiate and find a resolution in exchange for the lenders 'unwinding their exercise of remedies'. Two months of back and forth resulted in nothing. The suit claims that Raveendran's motive 'appears to have been to draw out negotiations to buy himself time to close on his prospective equity investments and other fundraising efforts'.

A raid by the Enforcement Directorate on Byju's in India spooked the lenders further. In April 2023, the Enforcement Directorate conducted searches and seizure action at three premises in Bengaluru in the case of Raveendran and his company Think & Learn under the provisions of the Foreign Exchange Management Act.

The ED said it had seized 'various incriminating documents and digital data'. A PTI report said the action was taken on the basis of 'various complaints' received from individuals and that Raveendran was issued 'several' summons, but he remained 'evasive and never appeared' before the ED. The company insisted that the ED visit 'was related to a routine inquiry under FEMA [FEMA is short for the Foreign Exchange Management Act, which governs the movement of capital in and out of India]' and that it was being 'completely transparent with the authorities and have provided them with all the information they have requested'. No further developments have occurred in this case as of the time of writing (September 2023).

Byju's didn't hold back in terms of legal responses once the lawsuit was filed against it. On 6 June, the company filed a counter complaint against lenders in the New York Supreme Court. It also refused to pay $40 million in interest. Byju's said that the lenders have 'concocted bogus events of default and purported to accelerate the entire outstanding debt, demanding payment in full from the Borrower and the guarantors under the Credit Agreement. The supposed events of default cannot possibly justify the acceleration of the debt. Inasmuch as they are breaches of the loan documents at all [and they are not], they are at most technical breaches of non-monetary provisions.'

After reading the 38-page complaint, there appear to be two sticking points. One, all the entities became guarantors to the loan except WhiteHat Jr, which became an issue. Two, Byju's could not provide audited financial results for 2021–22 by 27 September 2022 to the administrative agent.

There is an interesting juxtaposition of arguments here. Byju's says that the lenders were aware of the complications with the WhiteHat Jr guarantee. They were also aware that the audited earnings report for FY21 was delayed and until that was completed, the company could not start auditing the numbers for FY22. So the lenders were aware of the situation. By the same logic, the company should have been aware of what it was getting into in terms of breach of the terms of the debt agreement. One would expect that a company signing up for such a massive loan would do its due diligence before pledging a significant part of its business as collateral.

'Term loan B' refers to senior secured debt that is designed to be syndicated in the institutional loan market. It allows the borrower to make small repayments of the principal amount annually, while the bulk of the principal is payable at the termination of the loan. To reduce their risk, lenders tend to sell these loans ahead in secondary markets. Any uncertainty around the borrower's financial health makes lenders jittery. They offload as much as they can, making these loans cheaper in the secondary market. On 5–6 June 2023, the term loan was quoted at around 64.5 cents a dollar, according to Bloomberg data. In simple words, it means that investors didn't think that the company could repay its loans and were, therefore, assigning a 35% probability of default. That's where hedge funds or financiers who specialize in distressed debt buy these loans at discount. Byju's should surely have known this, since it's common practice.

The matter is still sub judice, even as both Byju's and the lenders are said to have been talking to find an out-of-court solution. There were reports that the two parties aimed to find a solution and finalize a new agreement on 3 August 2023, but, like before, nothing happened. All we know right now is that negotiations are going on. No more, no less.

But the tricky part is that the company seems to have accessed and utilized around half of the loan amount. This means it has to pay back half a billion dollars or more, plus interest and penalties if the loan is terminated. Byju's, by all estimates, doesn't have that kind of money. At this point, it appears it doesn't even have the means to raise that kind of funding.

If the pandemic years of 2020 and 2021 were marked by unbridled ambition and growth, 2022 was the year of reckoning and 2023 is when the chickens came home to roost.

———

I am writing this in September 2023 and from here, it looks like Byju's is in all kinds of trouble at home and abroad. Capital is hard to come by and the company is neck-deep in debt. It is facing an enquiry by the dreaded Enforcement Directorate. For it to sustain operations and come out of the mess, the businesses need to work and generate very high profits from operations. Which doesn't seem to be happening right now.

Everyone in the ecosystem – employees, investors, auditors, industry experts – believes the company is in a very tough spot. That is, everyone except its top management. What is helping them maintain an illusion is a lack of firm data.

It is impossible to get an accurate assessment of Byju's financial position because the company hasn't filed its audited earnings for FY22 and FY23. Even if you get the earnings report for FY23 (the period ended on 31 March 2023), it might not give you the real picture of things as they are right now. Six months, as we have seen in the past, is a long time in the start-up world.

I reached out to multiple people inside and outside the company to get a sense of where the business stands now. I have triangulated data and used the closest approximation I could get. This is not foolproof by any means, but it gives us a picture of where the business could be currently, according to the consensus opinions of many experts.

For ease of understanding, I have divided Byju's businesses into three parts: the core online learning, Byju's Tuition Centres and the acquisitions. Let's start with the first one.

Once the mainstay of the business, the core online learning business seems to be failing or at least losing growth momentum. This was inevitable. Raveendran saw it coming a while back. In an interview with *Business Today*'s Udayan Mukherjee in August 2021, he admitted as much. There are multiple reasons for this.

I will put the lack of clear learning outcomes topmost on the list. In the test-prep segment, for example, measuring learning outcomes is easy. You pick a test-prep company, online or offline, based on what you want to do. If it helps you crack the entrance tests you want to pursue, you have a positive learning outcome. It's similar with the upskilling or higher learning segments. These are need-based and focused approaches. The after-school supplementary learning is different. It is more holistic and, therefore, measuring learning outcomes becomes tricky.

Is higher marks in exams the benchmark for learning outcomes? Or understanding the fundamentals? Or just being able to express yourself? That's a level-one problem.

The second-level problem is, how do you measure what helped you gain any of this? There are many variables to

Why the order is... Byju's...

consider for students in this segment. Their learning is affected one way or another by the school, the teachers, peer learning, self-awareness, as well as the app/tutorial they are taking.

In most cases, it is a sum of all these factors that brings improvement in a child's academic performance. Now, some companies may have cracked this, but Byju's hasn't. There *(1)* is no way to conclusively prove that a student has become better or worse by using the company's app. *(2)*

The lack of personalization is another big issue. There is no mentor support, to begin with. Even with the app, there is a set template in which the questions appear. I used the app for a few weeks and there is no innovation or novelty whatsoever; nothing is custom-made for the user. Unsurprisingly, the return rate is high, because children lose interest after a point. The tablet becomes another device to play games on. *(3)*

Then there is reputational damage. By now, Byju's has become notorious for its predatory sales practices. Layoffs *(4?)* while spending big on advertising, and concerns around data safety and the effectiveness of the product have all combined to result in a negative perception.

By the end of July 2023, the online learning vertical was estimated to be logging a monthly run rate of around ₹150 crore, which is a revenue of around ₹1,800 crore for a year, with losses said to be running at 100% of revenue. Sales became increasingly difficult after the company moved to inside sales and fired thousands of salespersons. Returns are said to be higher at 25–30% from around 20% a year back. All in all, this division is said to be a mess. The company had hoped that the offline/hybrid business would lay the foundation for the next phase of growth, but that business too is unravelling fast.

———

Raveendran had perfected teaching in a room and at scale. He had found a market for both, and achieved great success. So, when he realized in 2021 that the future of edtech was coaching centres and launched Byju's Tuition Centre, it looked like it was destined for success. He was on home turf. He had the first-mover advantage. The business should have taken off with minimal effort.

Almost two years on, the tuition centre business is in tatters, I found while reporting. Thousands of employees have either left or been fired. The top leadership is gone. Many centres are running empty most of the week. Classes are being cancelled. New enrolments are proving difficult. Renewals, even more so. The business is bleeding money. It's like a boat with a million holes. How Raveendran made a mess of something that he understood so well remains a mystery. But this is what we know.

The first and the biggest problem is the lack of quality teachers. Teachers are the building blocks of a good coaching centre. It is their experience, teaching style and name that brings students to a centre. This is why even well-established coaching chains hire good teachers, pay them well and keep them in good humour.

Byju's Tuition Centre (BTC) works on a hub-and-spoke model for teachers. There is an expert teacher at a centralized location, taking the classes, and then there is another teacher, usually one with less experience, at each centre, to clear doubts, etc.

Multiple people who have been associated with the business almost since its start told me Byju's hires freshers, mostly from engineering backgrounds, as educators for the tuition centres. One of these joined eight months before his graduation results came. Salaries of the educators are the lowest among all white-collar employees, including people from the sales and marketing teams.

The academic heads at these centres make about ₹6–7 lakh per annum, compared with ₹8–9 lakh for marketing managers and ₹15–18 lakh for sales managers. It is surprising that Raveendran, who started off as a teacher, let this happen. It also shows where the company's focus is.

Naturally, the quality of education has suffered and, as a result, there have been many complaints from parents. Parents have also complained about the absence of teachers which has led to cancellations of classes, at times for weeks. It has become so bad that parents are coming to the centres and saying their children are watching videos on the PW app, one person who has been involved with the business told me. 'Parents say the PW app is free and the teachers explain the subjects better,' this person said. 'Education, like healthcare, runs on referrals. Imagine the kind of dissatisfaction when one parent can't give five referrals for BTC?'

Understandably, the renewals at BTC are poor. The renewal rate from 2022 is around 40%, but at least two-thirds of the renewals have happened at a discount of 50–65%. The pressure to renew subscriptions is so high that salespeople have been incessant in following up. The hard sell has driven parents up the wall.

The above are symptoms of a larger malaise afflicting Byju's, which, in a way, goes back to how the idea of BTC originated, and was scaled up. BTC, as a concept, came into existence in July 2021. Byju's opened many centres and built a very expensive and experienced team to run the business. At one time, there were more than 7,500 people in the tuition centre vertical. But there was a fundamental problem. Byju's focused on scale, thinking it would eventually bring sustainability. But the offline coaching business is difficult, requires a lot of patience, and needs a very brick-by-brick approach. You have to start with one centre, figure out the economics, bring the unit economics under control and only then expand.

But if you start with scale, you have to sell learning like a commodity, which is very difficult. More so for Byju's because of its multi-year contracts with parents. One of the biggest problems with edtech companies is that they treat education as a product whereas it is a service. Education can't be sold like chips or soap or any other fast-moving consumer good.

Raveendran was advised to take it slow, start with a handful of centres, understand the business and its challenges, make a playbook and then expand. But he had different ideas. The company was in a hurry. It had money in the bank. It was also desperate to find another avenue for growth. It wanted to move fast and scale at speed. It was the same reason why the tuition centre business wasn't merged with Aakash, despite the two businesses being similar, even complementary.

But all that hustle hasn't helped. At the end of July 2023, Byju's had 302 tuition centres, all bleeding money. Like the

(2)

online learning business, the tuition centre business also has wonky unit economics.

The average ticket size for a course at the tuition centres is ₹72,000. After deducting goods and services tax, finance costs, refunds and sales and marketing costs – which include salaries and incentives for sales and marketing teams, cost of marketing campaigns for centres, software and other allowances like travel – the contribution margin per unit is ₹2,935.

The average monthly revenue across the 302 BTC centres is ₹48 crore. The monthly contribution margin from the business is ₹2.12 crore, translating into ₹25.5 crore over a year. Here, too, a big part of the revenue is actually generated by Byju's giving loans to parents because lenders have stopped financing the company's products. So, essentially, the company is taking money from reserves, lending it to parents and showing it as revenues.

The monthly fixed cost per centre – rent, utility bills, salaries to academic staff and others except sales and marketing, etc. – is around ₹10 lakh. For the overall business, it is ₹30.2 crore. For the full year, this fixed cost amounts to ₹362 crore, capping the total loss from the tuition centre business at nearly ₹340 crore for a year if we adjust for the contribution margin.

The calculation above is done at the unit level. It, therefore, doesn't take into account overheads like the salaries of executives and business leaders who oversee multiple centres or managers. Add their salaries, and the hole grows deeper.

Just to break even on the unit level, every centre has to sell around 340 units every month. The average number of sales per centre per month was around 24 till June 2023. To push this to 340 units is not possible. How will they accommodate those many students in every centre?

To break even, costs will have to reduce very significantly. Even if sales start happening organically and centres operate at full capacity, the business will still struggle to do more than break even at the unit level. Fixed costs will still remain high, so the business will never be able to turn huge profits.

This is the reason why even the best offline coaching centres can only generate margins of 10–15% EBITDA (Earnings Before Interest Tax Depreciation and Amortization, which is often referred to as Operating Profit). This is why offline coaching centres are cost- and operations-heavy businesses and simply can't be run like a tech start-up.

In traditional offline coaching centres, there is a centre head who handles everything and all the verticals report to this person. At BTCs, however, three different verticals operate in silos. The sales team is disconnected from the marketing team, which is disconnected from the academics team. The centres are headed by the area business head who is from the marketing team. So, if a student comes with a problem to the centre head, he can't do anything.

The teachers report to the regional academic director. Salespeople would promise the moon, which the academic team can't deliver. So, when students come to the centres and get to know the real deliverables, there is a huge mismatch of expectations. The sales team doesn't understand academics, the business team isn't on the same page with sales. There is an enormous disconnect within the system.

As a result, many students say they don't want to continue

and want their money back. Anecdotal information suggests things have worsened in the past few months. For example, in many cases where students have been dissatisfied and have filed for refunds, the refunds have not been processed despite being approved. The company doesn't have the funds required. This has been escalating.

The refunds issue has escalated so much that the centre heads are afraid of coming to the centres. One person told me that there are police coming to one or the other centre every other day. Or centre heads are being called to the police stations. Or there are fights and arguments at the centres with students demanding refunds.

In the online business, if the customer had a problem, they would call the salesperson. The salesperson could switch off their phone or refuse to take the calls and the customers would have no recourse. The sales window would close in 14 days and then the customer could do nothing much. In the tuition centre business, however, the customer has a physical address to go to. So these centres are not only having to deal with dissatisfied tuition centre customers but also with unhappy customers who had bought online courses.

To make matters worse, the funding tap is closed. The brick-and-mortar coaching business at scale was a cash-guzzler by design, right off the blocks. Result? Cost cutting. Layoffs.

Things started falling apart with the resignation of the chief business officer Nishant Bhasin in June 2023. Harshit Chehal, who was heading post-sales customer service, also resigned at the same time. Thousands of people have been fired since. The total number of salespeople in the tuition centre business has been reduced to 900 from 2,400. The number of marketing managers is being reduced to 30 from over 300.

The post-sales team based in Gurugram, the marketing team headed by Jiten Mahendra, and the learning and development team headed by Indraneel Kumar Das were asked to leave. Many other senior executives with excellent pedigree and experience left on their own. Gurpreet Singh Sandhu, vice president of business, Siddhesh Joglekar, vice president of marketing, Hema Pachisia, HR head – the list is endless. Himanshu Bajaj, former head of consumer and retail practice for Asia at global consultancy firm Kearney, who was hired to lead Byju's Tuition Centre, told his team in July that he had put in his papers and was going on 'garden leave'.

As a result, Mohit, the de facto head of the India operations of Byju's, took charge. Mohit did what he knows best. Sales. Cost-cutting. He first combined the sales and marketing teams and then the post-sales service with academics and gave all powers to his sales team and made the area and zonal business heads, even the regional directors, report to the sales team. It caused friction and resulted in attrition. By July 2023, more than 3,000 people had quit.

As we went to publication, the news came through that Mohit had moved out of the company and Arjun Mohan was taking over as CEO. Raveendran maintained in an email to employees that Mohit was moving on for personal reasons and that his exit was a bittersweet moment for him. But 'it could be that Mohit was made the scapegoat for the debacle of the business', several industry watchers told me. This was inevitable.

BTC today is where Byju's always was. A hardcore, sales-driven organization. It had a great opportunity. It had the first-mover advantage. It had a great base. However, the lack of leadership and the apathy towards students and teachers has brought the offline business to a stage where its survival is in question.

Salaries have been delayed by weeks for a large number of people, month after month. Incentives haven't been paid since September 2022. The company doesn't have enough money to even pay utility bills or maintenance and run the centres properly. The local printer stopped doing job-work for BTC because he hadn't been paid. Employees have had to buy fuel for generators from their own pockets. The stationery vendor has not been paid. The annual maintenance contract with Daikin for the servicing of air conditioning has lapsed because of non-payment. The list goes on.

not paying bills

In one of the centres, people in the know told me, there are three washrooms. There are five urinals. Two of them haven't been working for months. Out of the two taps in a washroom, one doesn't work. Maintenance work in the washrooms is pending because vendors are not paid. Paper tissues have been discontinued in the name of cost-cutting. This is across centres. Inhuman, no? Who is responsible?

Now let's take a look at the acquisitions. Great Learning – acquired in 2021 – is currently looking at an annual revenue of ₹800–1,000 crore. This is in FY24. The other businesses in the US – Epic, Osmo and Tynker – are clocking a combined

US businesses

annual revenue of around ₹1,000 crore. None of these businesses are generating any money though. While Great Learning, Epic and Tynker are close to breaking even, Osmo is still deep in the red.

At home, WhiteHat Jr is a dead weight. It's been sitting like a black hole in Byju's balance sheet since the latter bought it for $300 million in August 2020. The mood had been different then. Edtech was growing rapidly, coding was the flavour of the season, and WhiteHat Jr was on fire.

Founder Karan Bajaj had had a great pitch. In an interview with the *Telegraph*, Bajaj, the former head of Discovery India, said that he had realized there was a 'massive gap between the skills needed in the new world and the curriculum in schools' when his two daughters started school. He decided to bridge the gap because in the future, 'jobs that don't require creation will be automated'. So, the focus must be on creation.

The pandemic gave the model legitimacy. Many people lost their jobs. But engineers were still in high demand because the world was running online. Coding became a life skill. WhiteHat Jr doubled down. Catch them young and teach them coding. It wanted to make children 'creators of technology rather than consumers of technology'. It found quite a few takers.

But in reality, this was yet another aggressive sales company, which created an illusion to market itself and its model. Remember Wolf Gupta? The same Wolf Gupta, who learnt AI and landed a job at Google. Do you remember how old he was then? Was he nine? Or 12? Or 13? Do you recall how much he earned? Was it ₹150 crore? Or ₹1.2 crore? Or $1.2 million?

At the time of the acquisition, WhiteHat Jr earned ₹84 crore in monthly revenue, half of which came from the US market. It had taken Bajaj $10 million (around ₹75 crore then) and 18 months to spin it into a business that recorded an annual revenue of nearly ₹1,000 crore. It was a dream run. It had made complete sense for Byju's to pay $300 million for the deal. It would have taken many months and millions of dollars to build a similar company and time was of the essence here.

There were many things that Byju's wanted desperately – live classes, outcomes, and access to and growth in the US market. Byju's was raising money at the valuation of almost 10 times the revenue. It could easily get a valuation bump of around $3 billion on WhiteHat Jr's revenue by paying $300 million. It looked like a no-brainer at the time.

But the coding company could never live up to the hype. It was always a tricky business to scale. One, live classes run on thin margins because there is a huge educator cost involved. Two, the customer acquisition cost is always very high. Coding is a skill, not a necessity, and there is no repeat customer. Three, coding was a pandemic business, the flavour of the season – a hobby if you like.

As schools reopened, things changed. One, children had very little time for activities outside school; everything that wasn't essential, including coding, took a back seat. Also because of the National Education Policy's focus on coding, many schools started their own courses in coding, rendering WhiteHat Jr redundant. So, the unit economics never worked.

It certainly didn't help that WhiteHat Jr was now embroiled in allegations of wrongful advertising and unethical practices. Also the stories of a work culture that was beyond toxic had started filtering out; the company also filed an unsuccessful defamation suit.

WhiteHat Jr had filed a ₹20 crore defamation suit against Pradeep Poonia, who had been, and still remains, one of the most vocal critics of WhiteHat Jr and Byju's, in the Delhi High Court in November 2020. The company alleged that Poonia was defaming and spreading misinformation about the start-up. It also blamed him for infringing trademarks by using a YouTube handle named WhiteHat Sr. In less than six months, it withdrew the suit.

The only way to reduce burn at WhiteHat Jr is to stop spending on customer acquisition, which, in turn, will reduce the overall business. It is a Catch-22 situation. The reality is that the company, in its past or current iteration, will never make a single dime in profit.

From the date of acquisition, according to Byju's FY21 earnings report, WhiteHat Jr contributed ₹326.66 crore of total revenue and ₹1,548.76 crore to losses before tax from operations. The meteoric rise and dramatic fall of WhiteHat Jr is a future management case study.

Since Bajaj left, there have been talks about Byju's shutting it down. But Raveendran told me multiple times that the company is 'changing it [WhiteHat Jr] for organic growth', without any further explanation.

Both Raveendran and Gokulnath have been insistent on keeping the brand alive. Days before *TechCrunch* reported in February 2023 that the coding company was going to shut down, Gokulnath told me how deeply and personally they were connected with the brand. Their child is a coder and, as a parent, she said she couldn't shut down the brand because thousands of children would be left in the lurch. And then there are educators.

In conversations over many months, whenever I asked him about WhiteHat Jr, Raveendran admitted that there had been pressure but that he would never shut down the brand. His responses were always along the lines of this: WhiteHat Jr employs 12,000 women educators, a majority of whom are the sole breadwinners of their families, and he can't render them jobless. In his words, it was an ode to the socialist fabric of the society in Kerala where he grew up. Full marks for integrity and commitment. I only wish he had had the same integrity and commitment towards the tens of thousands of Byju's employees whom the company has fired in the last year or so.

WhiteHat Jr has now diversified into teaching maths, music and arts too. But it hasn't changed the company's fortunes. At the end of July 2023, it was clocking a monthly run rate of ₹25–30 crore, less than one-third of what it was making at the time of its acquisition, with a similar amount in net losses.

As things stand now, WhiteHat Jr is a dead horse. There's no point flogging it anymore. The founder knew that three years ago. So he happily took his hundreds of millions of dollars and is now living in Goa, reportedly thinking about a new venture in solar financing. His pitch has changed. As has his audience. He is no longer worried about the future of children or jobs. He has made his millions. And Byju's is stuck with a lemon.

Aakash is a different beast altogether. The horse, presumably dead a couple of summers ago, has found a new lease of life and is galloping ahead, at a tearing pace. If numbers are to be believed – and this is just guesstimates made by credible sources because we have no way to be sure till the financials are officially filed – the company logged around ₹2,300 crore in revenue in FY23, with around ₹400 crore in profit. You would think this would be the silver lining in Byju's story right now. It could have been if it weren't mismanaged. Let's start from the beginning.

Byju's acquired Aakash for ₹6,820 crore, in a 70:30 cash–stock split. In such large acquisitions, the cash is paid out in tranches. In June 2021, when the deal was closed, the Chaudhry family – the founders – got some of the cash component. Blackstone Group, which held about 37% of Aakash before the deal, did not take any money at the time due to tax issues that would be related to capital gains. The final payment to the Chaudhry family and Blackstone was due in June 2022. But a lot of things happened before that.

It is common knowledge that neither the Chaudhrys nor Blackstone was interested in the Byju's deal at first. But Raveendran pursued them. At the time, the talk was about creating synergies and growing together. Byju's had unmatched sales machinery and exponential growth. AESL had pedagogy, a stellar track record and a healthy balance sheet. But it lacked momentum. Coming together would seemingly have helped both companies, Aakash Chaudhry, then managing director, said in an interview with The Morning Context in April 2021. He didn't want his company to be the Kodak equivalent of education. So, he persuaded his father and a deal was reached.

Unfortunately, things didn't pan out as hoped as Raveendran focused entirely on increasing his company's valuation. Byju's raised $1.5 billion in a matter of months, and its valuation rose to $15 billion from $12 billion at the time of the Aakash deal.

Byju's, however, didn't make a move to integrate Aakash into its operations. Aakash decided to go ahead with getting ready for integration anyway. The company identified people in teams such as finance, human resources and marketing, and asked them to make a blueprint. But they realized soon that Byju's universe was a unified mass of chaos. There was nothing to integrate with.

The finance team found Byju's didn't have a CFO. There was no chain of command and no clear direction. When the HR team started to draw up a roadmap for integration, it realized that everyone in the top brass at Byju's had their own HR team. One group of HR people didn't know another group. Again, there was no chain of command. Everything was in disarray. The worst was the sales and marketing team. Everyone knew about their practices – overpromising, underdelivering, mis-selling – and it still came as a shock.

After evaluating integration on many fronts for around six months, Aakash gave up. Instead of working together, Aakash and Byju's became two separate silos.

Back when the lockdown was in full force, Byju's had overhired. But after the world started opening up, sales went down. Byju's had more people than they had work. It tried to reposition the surplus sales reps in its subsidiaries, including Aakash. Two things happened as a result. One, Byju's sales team cannibalized Aakash's sales. Two, bad practices became endemic because of Byju's salespeople.

Byju's salespeople reportedly started doing weird underhanded deals with Aakash's salespeople. They bought Aakash's leads for 2x the incentive Aakash was giving its salespersons and then sold the courses themselves and got a fat incentive. This was because the incentives paid at Byju's were multiples of the incentive at Aakash. This internal scam was a nice merry-go-round while it lasted.

Meanwhile, the top management of the two companies were singing completely different tunes. The leadership team at Aakash was so disconnected from the decision-makers at Byju's that they were not even part of discussions over the fundraising, IPO, etc., even though these were about Aakash!

June 2022 arrived amid all this chaos. Byju's told the other two parties that there was a liquidity problem and it couldn't settle the agreed tranche of payment. There was a lot of back and forth and a lot of heartburn. The money was finally paid between July and September 2022. But here's the catch. It didn't come from Byju's parent company Think & Learn as it should have, but from a Singapore company created by Raveendran.

Before we get any further, it is important to understand the corporate structure Raveendran built in Singapore. Between 2020 and 2022, Raveendran started four companies in Singapore that we know of:

- Byju's Pte Ltd
- Byju's Investments Pte Ltd
- Byju's Global Pte Ltd
- Byju's Holdings 1 Pte Ltd

Two of the companies – Byju's Pte Ltd and Byju's Investments Pte Ltd – are non-exempt private companies, while the other two are exempt private companies. An exempt private company in Singapore faces relatively less red tape and fewer government regulations. Its limitations are that there cannot be more than 20 shareholders, and that none of the shareholders can be a corporate entity; only individuals are allowed.

Such a company has some advantages. There's a three-year partial corporate tax exemption, for example. Unlike other structures, exempt private companies can also extend loans to their directors.

Small, exempt private companies are also eligible to be exempted from having their accounts audited; they just have to meet two of these three criteria:

- annual revenue should not exceed $10 million
- total assets should not exceed $10 million at the end of the fiscal year
- a maximum of 50 employees at the end of the fiscal year

Now, let's examine each of the companies and their businesses. First up is Byju's Pte Ltd.

It was incorporated on 14 January 2020 as a regular private limited company, and it is 100% owned by Think & Learn. According to documents obtained from Singapore's Accounting and Corporate Regulatory Authority, or ACRA, Byju's Pte Ltd is listed as a holding company. Through this company, Think & Learn owns a 59.52% majority stake in Great Learning Education Pte Ltd, an online higher education provider. The document also shows it has two registered charges on 26 November 2021 from GLAS Trust

Company LLC, a UK-based multinational non-bank loan agency. A charge is a form of security interest usually taken by a lender or creditor to secure repayment of a loan.

For the year 2022, Byju's Pte Ltd reported sales of $30.23 million.

Byju's Investments Pte Ltd was incorporated on 10 May 2022 as a regular private limited company and it is 100% owned by Byju's Global Pte Ltd (which comes next on our list of Singapore entities). According to documents obtained from ACRA, Byju's Investments Pte Ltd is listed as a holding company, just like Byju's Pte Ltd.

Byju's Global Pte Ltd was registered on 6 May 2022 as an exempt private limited company. It is 100% owned by Raveendran. It is listed on the ACRA website as a holding company. It has two charges: On 29 September from Qatar Holding LLC (owned by the Qatar Investment Authority) and on 26 October from Internet Fund V Pte Ltd (a Tiger Global investment vehicle). This means the company has raised debt and the lenders have placed charges on some assets that have been pledged to secure this credit. We could not ascertain the amount of debt raised in these two cases.

On 7 September 2022, Byju's Investments Pte Ltd passed a resolution to change its constitution, creating a charge on its shares by its holding company, Byju's Global Pte, towards the Qatar Investment Authority. The amendments put QIA in a superior position. One of the amendments allows QIA to transfer mortgaged shares at its discretion. The current shareholder cannot dispose of those shares unless the charge is cleared.

Finally, let's look at Byju's Holdings 1 Pte Ltd. It was registered on 31 August 2022. Like Byju's Global Pte Ltd, this company is also registered as an exempt private company and owned 100% by Raveendran.

Note that Raveendran is the only shareholder in Byju's Holdings 1 Pte Ltd as well as in Byju's Global Pte Ltd and, by extension, Byju's Investments Pte Ltd. Also note that the two companies where he has a 100% direct shareholding are both exempt private companies. The documentation from ACRA makes it apparent that except for Byju's Pte (the Think & Learn subsidiary that holds a majority stake in Great Learning), none of the other companies seem to have any business or revenue model. But Byju's Global and Byju's Holdings 1 Pte have invested a lot of capital in Byju's parent company in India, Think & Learn.

There is no clarity on how capital is being moved between the companies in Singapore and India. Had any capital gone from India to the companies in Singapore? The Reserve Bank of India's regulations ban moving capital out of India in order to invest the same funds from abroad in a related Indian entity. So, how did the two Singapore companies owned by Raveendran raise money in the first place and where did that capital come from?

'It is improbable that money was lent with no collateral such as a charge on the company,' a Singapore-based accountant told me when I was reporting for this story. 'Unless there is a side agreement where the promoter has pledged his shares to the new investor/lender. This may be ripe for a FEMA violation. But that is speculative.'

As things turned out, the final payments for the Aakash deal came from Byju's Investments. As a result, the Singapore company – and by extension, Raveendran, since he is the only shareholder in its parent company – held about 27% stake in Aakash. Also, remember that this final payment happened around September 2022.

Remember, Byju's Global, the parent company of Byju's Investments, had two charges from Qatar Holding LLC and Internet Fund V Pte Ltd. This means the company has raised debt, and the lenders have placed charges on some assets that have been pledged to secure this credit, and as we admitted above, we could not ascertain the amount of debt raised in the two cases.

The cheques paid for the Aakash deal had barely cleared when Aakash received a demand for ₹300 crore in an unsecured loan from Byju's. This was around October 2022. The company wasn't prepared for this.

When the loan request came in, Aakash did not have much free cash. At that point, it had around Rs ₹350 crore in the bank – the advance payment made by students – which was meant for paying salaries. Taking out ₹300 crore would mean a significant depletion of money in the bank. But Byju's did it. Things came to a breaking point in January, but Aakash was able to avert a catastrophe.

In the meantime, Raveendran's efforts to raise fresh capital went in vain and the business started crumbling under its own weight. Raveendran told me that the Chaudhrys suggested an IPO for Aakash. That business was doing well after the pandemic. A potential public offering could unlock its real potential and give Byju's some much-needed capital.

But it would still have taken months and Byju's needed money now.

The sought-after capital finally arrived in May 2023. But it wasn't an equity investment. Byju's raised ₹2,000 crore (around $250 million) in structured debt from the US-based investment fund, Davidson Kempner Capital Management. The three-year loan facility was raised through a combination of non-convertible debentures and a smaller portion of compulsorily convertible debentures, secured against the future cash flows of Aakash. I was wondering why a company like Davidson Kempner would be interested in Byju's when we got a tip in July 2023 that the investment fund had accused Byju's of financial misconduct, and taken control over Aakash Educational Services Ltd and its accounts.

This is what I discovered while investigating the tip. Byju's accessed ₹400 crore from the ₹2,000 crore loan. The rest of the money was held in an escrow account, which the company could not immediately tap. I learnt that Byju's took out around ₹100 crore from the rest of the loan and tried to show the account was untouched. It wasn't clear how Byju's was able to withdraw money held in escrow, which it wasn't supposed to. This is also the contention of Davidson Kempner's accusation of financial misconduct being committed at the company.

Sometime between April 2023 and Davidson Kempner taking over the accounts at Aakash, Byju's took out another ₹300 crore from the test prep company's operational account. Just like it did around October 2022. Only, this time, there was no explanation, no demands, and no filings made to the ministry of corporate affairs. This huge withdrawal was set to create another cash-crunch like in January 2023, when Aakash was struggling to pay salaries.

In the offline coaching business, revenue is front-loaded, which means it comes at the beginning of a session. Admissions happen between May and July. It is the time when these companies are most cash-rich, since students pay the entire course fee.

By November, the revenue stops coming and the coaching centre coasts along with only expenses till March. The good thing is that these are predictable fixed costs and overheads like salaries, rent, utility bills, etc. Coaching centres can plan ahead so that they have enough funds to pay salaries during these lean months. But the system breaks down if there is a sudden outflow of large amounts of cash as in this instance.

This is not viable for a 10% EBITDA business. It is possible, even likely, that Davidson Kempner's move to take control of Aakash's operational account came after the latest cash withdrawal from Byju's. I have seen internal documentation, suggesting Byju's has an outstanding loan of Rs 1,326 crore from Aakash as of 4 September 2023. This could be the loan amount that came from Davidson Kempner, plus the unsecured loan Byju's took from the test-prep company.

Now you may well ask, how could Davidson Kempner take control of Aakash's accounts? What leverage does it have and what are the implications? For that, we have to see what was happening in Singapore.

A couple of months before raising the debt from the American investment fund, on 23 March 2023 to be exact, Raveendran incorporated Beeaar Investco Pte. Ltd, a fifth company in that country, which we know about. This was also 100% owned by him. Sometime between then and 15 May, Raveendran transferred the Aakash stake held by Byju's Investments to Beeaar Investco.

When I learnt this, two questions came to my mind. One, why and how was this done? And two, if the eventual beneficiary is Raveendran in both cases, what is the need to create one more company and make things more complicated?

Generally, you create such complicated structures to obfuscate and thus buy time, which in this case Byju's used to try and raise more funds. Remember the charge from QIA on Byju's Global, and Byju's Investments' resolution to change its constitution? Now, if the QIA charge was related to Byju's Investments' stake in Aakash, the resolution makes it clear that the current shareholder cannot dispose of those shares unless the charge is cleared. So how did Beeaar Investco get hold of the identical stake in Aakash as Byju's Investments? The only explanation is that the shares were transferred from the latter to the former. How Raveendran managed to transfer shares without clearing the charge – if the charge was related to Aakash's shares – remains a mystery.

Byju's Singapore Companies

Company	Ownership	Investments
Byju's Pte (BPTE)	Byju's owns 100%	Owns 59.52% in Great Learning
Byju's Global Pte (BGPTE)	Byju Raveendran owns 100%	–
Byju's Investment Pte (BIPTE)	Byju's Global Pte owns 100%	₹1,894 crore in Byju's; ₹2,000 crore to Blackstone and Aakash promoters

Company	Ownership	Investments
Byju's Holding Pte (BHPTE)	Byju Raveendran owns 100%	₹1,220 crore in Byju's
Beeaar Investco Pte	Byju Ravindran owns 100%	Owns 27% in Aakash, which was previously held by BIPTE

Sources: Business profile documents of the companies accessed via ACRA

Now, in large debt deals like the one between Byju's and Davidson Kempner, lenders want security against their investments. The only collateral Byju's could have offered was the shares Raveendran held in Aakash, but there might already have been be a charge on them. An innovative workaround was reached.

Two people close to the development told me that Byju's agreement with Davidson Kempner is a power of attorney. Technically, Byju's couldn't sell a stake or take a pledge on Aakash's shares without the approval of the Chaudhrys and Blackstone. So it seems the company found a roundabout way. What this did though, is make the ownership of Aakash very complicated.

Davidson Kempner has a power of attorney on that stake of Aakash, nearly 27%, which is held by Raveendran through his Singapore company. Also, remember, the original deal for Aakash was a cash and stock deal. After the cash payouts, the Chaudhry family was left with an 18% stake in the test prep company while Blackstone had about 12%.

The messy state of affairs has led to another deadlock. Nearly 30 months into the deal, the Aakash acquisition is still incomplete. The Chaudhry family and Blackstone have been able to resist a merger or share swap so far.

According to news reports, Byju's had invoked the unconditional fallback agreement and issued a notice to the Chaudhry family, requesting the execution of the swap deal, in March 2023. The company wanted to consolidate ownership of Aakash, which had become a cash cow for it.

As a conclusion to the back and forth that followed, Blackstone and the Chaudhrys issued statements to Byju's that they would not be proceeding with the merger and fallback agreement. The Chaudhrys have told Byju's that they are terminating their merger and fallback agreement. Blackstone has also dragged its feet on moving ahead with the share swap, saying it is not contractually obligated to execute the share swap in T&L.

The move isn't surprising, given the change in fortunes of the two companies. While Aakash's revenue has nearly tripled since its acquisition, Byju's valuation was slashed by its largest shareholder, Dutch-listed technology investor Prosus, first to $6 billion in November last year and then to $5.1 billion in June.

Swapping their stake in Aakash for a stake in Byju's would mean the Chaudhry family will own less than 1% in Byju's, which is not worth much. Clearly, neither the Chaudhry family nor Blackstone are interested in a share swap. Byju's wants this desperately, however. Aakash is the only cash-generating part of the business and it makes sense to own it completely. Also, without the swap, there is a real chance that Byju's will lose the controlling stake in the test-prep company.

Remember that Aakash's accounts are still controlled by Davidson Kempner. When Byju's took out money, which it wasn't supposed to, from Aakash, it constituted a technical default. After taking over the accounts, the investment fund asked Byju's to return the funds it accessed. Raveendran sought time. But that deadline passed without any repayment. Davidson Kempner could now decide to take the 27% stake in Aakash instead. If that happens and the investment fund teams up with the Chaudhrys and Blackstone, Byju's will lose control of Aakash. There are talks of Ranjan Pai, the co-founder of Aarin Capital, which was Byju's earliest backer, investing money, but even if that happens, Pai would want a stake in Aakash and he may even want to cut Raveendran out of the equation. This is another part of the business that is all over the place and all results are possible. We have to wait and watch to see how things unfold.

Aakash was Byju's only hope. Unlocking its potential was one way out of misery for Byju's. It indicated as much, first by announcing that it would take Aakash public separately and then by setting a mid-2024 timeline for this IPO. But increasingly, it is looking like Byju's could not only lose control of its most prized asset, but that this could also spiral into an existential crisis. This may be an opportune moment to look at the numbers again.

———

If you put everything together, that is about ₹6,500–7,000 crore in revenue, at the most optimistic assessment, for FY24, with only Aakash making any profit. This is after

Byju's has stopped all marketing expenses, including the sponsorship of the Indian cricket team, and cut costs wherever possible.

Given that it has raised around $3.5 billion since the pandemic – and approximately $6 billion overall – and grown in valuation to a mind-boggling $22 billion, Byju's doesn't have much to show if this is the state of affairs.

I did some back-of-the-envelope calculations to guesstimate what the company's revenues could be in FY22 and FY23. Remember, Raveendran had been talking about a turnover of ₹10,000 crore in FY22 when he gave an interview to *Business Today* in August 2021. I still remember his words: '. . . let me under-promise and overdeliver'. Well, ₹10,000 crore looks far away from reality now.

In effect, what Raveendran did by announcing that number was dig a hole for himself. Given the carnage after the FY21 earnings were released, the company is under tremendous pressure to show better numbers. More so because it kept stressing that about 40% of the revenue had been deferred to FY22 due to the auditor's insistence on a change in revenue recognition norms.

Everyone I have spoken with over the last year has estimated that the numbers for FY22 will be worse than FY21. So, you can understand Byju's predicament and the delay in filing the audited earnings.

The audit process itself didn't begin till June 2023, according to sources in Byju's, and this led Deloitte Haskins & Sells to resign as Byju's auditor. Byju's announced the appointment of BDO Global as the statutory auditor on the same day, but the resignation letter from Deloitte is telling.

The financial statements of the Company for the year ended March 31, 2022 are long delayed. In accordance with the Companies Act, 2013, the audited financial statements for the year ended March 31, 2022 were due to be laid before shareholders in the Annual General Meeting by September 30, 2022. We have also not received any communication on the resolution of the audit report modifications in respect of the year ended March 31, 2021, status of audit readiness of the financial statements and the underlying books and records for the year ended March 31, 2022 and we have not been able to commence the audit as on date. As a result, there will be significant impact on our ability to plan, design, perform and complete the audit in accordance with the applicable auditing standards.

The audit firm also pointed out that it had been writing to Raveendran since the end of September 2022 (November was the deadline for filing financial statements for the fiscal year ended 31 March 2022). Deloitte followed up with reminders in November and December 2022, and then March 2023.

Deloitte's resignation letter validated the statement from the lenders of the term loan in the US – and contradicted what Byju's had told the New York Supreme Court in its countersuit against its lenders. 'Although it has not yet been completed, progress has been made on the FY22 Audit, and no issues have been identified with it to date.'

Around the same time, Prosus's Russell Dreisenstock, Peak XV's managing director G.V. Ravishankar, and the Chan-Zuckerberg Initiative's Vivian Wu all quit the Byju's board without citing any reasons. This is, to say the least of it, unusual. The auditor – one of the world's biggest and best – quits and does so with a damning letter. Three major investors pull their representatives from the board. It is bound to raise questions about corporate governance.

Byju's response? The company first denied the exit of board members as unverified information and speculation, *more lies* and then claimed that the exits had been planned beforehand.

However, in separate statements, Prosus and Peak XV have confirmed that their representatives quit the edtech company's board because of the differences with the company's leadership. In a strongly worded statement, Prosus said that Byju's leadership regularly 'disregarded advice and recommendations relating to strategic, operational, legal, and corporate governance matters'. 'The decision for our director to step down from the Byju's board was taken after it became clear that he was unable to fulfil his fiduciary duty to serve the long-term interests of the company and its stakeholders,' read the Prosus statement.

Along similar lines, Peak XV Partners, the edtech firm's second-largest investor, told its limited partners that Byju's leadership was unwilling to follow advice and suggestions on corporate affairs as well as legal and operational matters given by Ravishankar. It also cited the company's lack of transparency in keeping investors updated on its state of affairs.

Today, Byju's is an empty shell of its glorious past. It has lost the confidence of parents, students, employees, investors and auditors. It is a trainwreck.

The $22 billion question is: where does it go from here?

11

Injury Time

So, what's next for Byju's and edtech?

Byju's back is against the wall and sometime in the next 6–12 months the fate of the company will be determined. Is this the beginning of the end for India's largest start-up? Or do Raveendran and his team have enough left in the tank to make a comeback, and rise from the ashes like a Phoenix?

That is a $22 billion question and the answer is neither easy nor straightforward. In many ways, Byju's has always been a one-man show, even though that's an odd way to characterize a company that had 50,000 employees and many stakeholders.

When the business decisions and gambles Raveendran took worked, they catapulted Byju's to a sequence of peaks and redefined the edtech industry. The flip side of the coin is, of course, that his decisions also resulted in the current trainwreck. The future of Byju's will surely rest on his decisions and actions (or inactions).

What options does he now have?

Given the situation Byju's finds itself in and the kind of

problems it faces, there aren't too many options left. Perhaps the most pragmatic thing would be to raise a down round, which means look for a fresh round of equity funding at a lower valuation than the last round.

Byju's is in dire need of substantial funds and no one would be willing to invest at the last valuation of $22 billion. A down round, therefore, seems the most sensible option. But it would require setting aside egos and thinking cool-headedly about the future of the company and of its customers and students. It would be safe to assume that the idea must have been tossed around during board meetings.

But here's the thing: private markets hate downrounds. Investment firms – VCs, PEs, and the like – don't like it, because this forces them to write down their investments. So, the unwritten rule about private markets is that start-up valuations are set in stone and can't go down. Entrepreneurs also dislike down rounds because they reduce the worth of promoter equity significantly, and, therefore, erode their net worth. So, you can understand why no one wants to take this route even if this seems to be the most viable one.

The lack of visibility about the business makes matters even worse for Byju's. No one knows the real state of the business. The company hasn't filed its financials for FY22 and FY23 and, in the absence of financial data, taking any bet on the company is like playing blind man's buff in a sandstorm. To add to the mistrust, the management (mostly Raveendran himself) has publicly made many misleading or over-optimistic claims about the company – '$300 million in a week', 'doubling revenues in FY21', 'only 2,500 layoffs', flip-flop around the investors quitting its board, etc.

Given a fluid business situation and a lot of make-believe from the founders, investors would be wary. But a down round could happen. If it's set at the right valuation, the market will clear.

That said, any money raised and spent on the business in its current iteration might be like throwing good money after bad. It's become clear that the business model and work culture need drastic changes if the core business of online learning and offline coaching centres is ever to make money. Any investor who's willing to buy into Byju's is likely to demand a re-engineering of the company.

Another option is to start selling off assets to pay off debts and streamline the balance sheet and take stock of whatever is left once the liabilities are wiped off. The *Economic Times* reported in September that Byju's is in talks to sell two of its assets – Epic and Great Learning – and thus raise up to $1 billion to repay the $1.2 billion term loan.

But this may be easier said than done and it still might not be enough to put the company back on a sustainable footing. Byju's went on a buying spree during the pandemic when the market was riding high. Edtech became the only game in town if students were to continue learning and, therefore, the demand for it shot through the roof.

In October 2023, lenders of the $1.2 billion term loan appointed risk advisory firm Kroll to protect assets at both Great Learning Education Pte. and the edtech firm's Singapore entity Byju's Pte. Ltd. Kroll, in turn, placed Great Learning into receivership in Singapore and replaced certain Byju's board members with its own representatives, according to Bloomberg.

The boom during the pandemic made investors look at India's 250 million students and take a top-down decision to invest in the industry. Interest rates were at zero and, therefore, liquidity was not a problem. Byju's, and it was by no means the only start-up to do so, raised cash at much higher valuations than it objectively deserved. Moreover, because it had a big war chest, Byju's also overpaid for all of its acquisitions.

Two years later, the market has turned on its head. Demand for online learning is depressed, there isn't enough liquidity in the financial system, and valuations are taking a beating across sectors, across markets. In the prevailing bearish conditions, it is anyone's guess how much cash a fire sale of assets can generate. It would be safe to assume that the company and its investors will have to take a haircut and a shave – a very deep discount – if there's a fire sale.

If this does happen, it could well be the biggest write down ever in India's start-up industry. Byju's would also be in conflict with investors who have bailed it out at various points while keeping the valuation intact. A most recent example would be the $250 million fundraise in September 2022, in which existing investors, including Qatar Investment Authority, Tiger Global and others, bought fresh equity at a $22 billion valuation.

However, the continuing financial crisis and the lack of transparency have forced even its most committed backers to cut valuations. In the absence of audited financial reports, people will also assume the worst.

A fire sale will put all the investors in a difficult situation because the valuation of what they own – stakes in Byju's

– will fall significantly. As of July 2023, Great Learning was looking at an annual revenue of ₹800–1,000 crore. The US businesses – Epic, Osmo and Tynker – were clocking a combined annual revenue of around ₹1,000 crore. A back-of-the-envelope calculation would put the revenue earned by Great Learning and Epic at around ₹1,200 crore or around $140 million.

Byju's last reported audited revenue was ₹2,280 crore in 2020–21 (around $310 million at April 2021 exchange rates). Around the same time, the company's valuation was $15 billion. Byju's raised funds throughout the Covid-19 pandemic, claiming to generate a likely revenue of ₹10,000 crore, or $1.3 billion, in 2021–22. So, its valuation around April 2021 was 48 times the actual revenue and 12 times the projected revenue. Calculating backwards using the same logic, the sale of Great Learning and Epic will wipe off nearly $2 billion from the valuation.

On 4 November 2023, Byju's released a three-paragraph press statement with partial financials for the year ended 31 March 2022 (FY22). Think & Learn reported 'a robust 2.3x growth to reach a total income of Rs 3,569 crore up from Rs 1552 crore in the previous year (FY21)' in its core business, excluding acquisitions. The EBITDA loss was down from ₹2,406 crore (FY21) to ₹2,253 crore.

Even these partial numbers are 20 months late. Second, the sales model changed towards end of calendar 2022, and the effects will mostly show up in 2022–23 and beyond. Consolidated numbers would have given a much clearer picture.

The standalone numbers also suggest disappointing

growth. It seems very unlikely that Raveendran's claims of generating a revenue of ₹10,000 crore in FY22 were achieved.

'I still don't understand how Byju managed to bring in investors at $22 billion,' says an edtech executive, requesting anonymity. 'What were they [the investors] thinking? Which edtech company will give them an exit at $66 billion [assuming a VC wants at least three times the return]? Investors are in for a bloodbath at this point. The value destruction will be unprecedented.'

An IPO sounds like a distant dream now. Byju's is under the scanner of multiple agencies, including the Enforcement Directorate, which is examining it for alleged foreign exchange violations. Given issues about corporate governance and compliance, exacerbating the financial crisis at the company, a public offer looks impossible in any realistic timeframe.

In fact, the way things are going, the planned IPO for Aakash also looks to be in jeopardy. No equity investment has come Byju's way in nearly a year and debts are ballooning.

Can Byju's be sold, lock, stock and barrel plus or minus the Raveendrans?

It is a running concern and there is general consensus among insiders and industry watchers that there is still value in the company. However, that value would translate into market valuations at way below the current levels. Adjusting to factor in the current problems, no one will be willing to put up more than $4–$5 billion for the entire business (around Prosus's valuation of $5.1 billion). That would be a value erosion of nearly 80%. But if Byju's can't quickly find a way out of this chakravyuha, the company could crumble and cease to be a running concern. That would drive the value down closer to zero.

———

I spoke with more than 10 people about the company's best future course of action. They were edtech entrepreneurs, educationists and experts who have been involved in or have been watching the industry for at least a decade or more. The sentiment is unanimous. Byju's will have to go through multiple surgeries and a lot of pain to survive this existential crisis and it doesn't have much time left since it's bleeding every day.

The first order of business will be to sort out the deep financial mess it is in. Once it can do that, Byju's will need a professional management team to figure out the next steps. A company of its size and scale can't work with an absentee founder, or with a de-facto chief who has no experience in management and runs the company like a zamindar.

Byju's is probably the only company of its scale in the world which lacks professional management. Its top leadership consists of Raveendran's family members and early students who have not worked for even a day outside the company, and therefore have no broader management experience.

The only exceptions are Arjun Mohan, who came back as CEO in September, and Ajay Goel who joined Byju's in April 2023 as chief financial officer after that post remained vacant for over 18 months. Goel quit on 24 October, while the FY22 earnings were said to be just around the corner. The timing of his exit and his barely seven-month-long stint raised several questions. He was replaced by Nitin Golani, a chartered accountant by training and an old hand at Byju's, in the interim. Something doesn't add up. Only time will tell. How no one on the board, including the investors' representatives, has ever raised questions about such a casual and nepotistic arrangement is beyond me, but I digress.

Once there is a professional management team in place, the company will need to think through its product and offerings. It is clear that both its core offerings – the online learning product and the offline tuition centres – are struggling. Byju's was the poster child of online learning in India. It was also the first mover in the offline space. It spent a fortune on becoming a household name.

But the company couldn't capitalize on the first-mover advantage and the brand it built and translate that into big profit margins. The company needs to go back to the drawing board, re-examine all its processes, and design products and services that not only work but for which customers are willing to pay enough for it to keep a margin.

If it is able to do all of this, and this is a big if, the company might just survive. The fundamental issues bedevilling the Indian education system haven't changed. This means there is still a space, maybe a big space, for online education to plug the gaps.

There is yet another problem to address and that might be the elephant in the room. Byju's is facing a raft of problems because there is a larger question of integrity and that goes right back to the founder.

From lenders to investors, everyone has questioned the integrity of the founder. People at the company, including its advisory council members, are stepping around this issue and the company cannot recover unless this is addressed squarely.

Lenders of the term loan B put this question of integrity at the centre of their plea in the lawsuit they filed against Byju's in Delaware in May. Davidson Kempner also raised the same question when it accused the company of financial misconduct. Employees and parents have been questioning it informally for years now.

One of the fundamental problems in the Byju's saga has been the overblown stories and projections. Imagine an entrepreneur telling investors he is creating a $100 billion company. He assures them that the company's revenue will be $1 billion this year and double every successive year. He shows them how his business is well on the way to becoming a $100 billion company on a spreadsheet and then he asks them if they want to be a part of this.

The entrepreneur goes on creating such scenarios on spreadsheets and gets more rounds of funding. He keeps telling investors that the business is making money and is very close to profitability and public listing. Rinse. Repeat. This continues for years until the market turns bearish and then the company declares losses that are twice the entire revenue and then everyone wakes up from this happy dream.

Many industry watchers don't visualize Byju's as a company fallen into bad times that might be able to turn it around. They see Byju's as a company that has deliberately chosen to mislead everyone, and incidentally made the founders very rich during this process.

Remember, its promoters – founder Byju Raveendran, his brother Riju Ravindran and Byju's wife, Divya Gokulnath – have together sold shares worth around $408.53 million in 40 secondary transactions since 2015, according to a recent analysis by PrivateCircle Research.

Raveendran has to come clean and maybe take a step back in terms of ceding operational control if the company is to find a white knight. Investors in the company not only created a bubble, but by focusing on Byju's and the like at inflated valuations, they also contributed to a lot of smaller players becoming collateral damage.

Where does Indian edtech go from here?

That's a broader question, but it rises naturally.

Byju's and other edtech companies identified a gap in the Indian education system and offered a tech solution to bridge the learning gap. Sadly, after years of building edtech 2.0 and spending billions of investors' dollars, that learning gap still exists. The after-school supplemental education model is not dead. There is no way 100 million children or more can do without it.

The reality is that this learning gap has widened over the years and it worsened during the pandemic when lower-income students couldn't afford the broadband connection and the smartphones and laptops required to access online learning. Parents still need after-school supplemental education to help their children get ahead. They need it even more today than they needed it 20 years ago. Yes, the

Byju's model of edtech might have failed, but the problem still exists, and the market will evolve and create new solutions for it.

As the market reboots and the dust settles on edtech 2.0, the biggest collective learning has been that edtech in its current iteration isn't any more efficient than the offline tuition centres that have existed for decades. The promise of online learning was to disrupt education.

But over the last decade, it evolved into just an online extension of the existing offline model, with the technology providing more reach. Reach is good but it's not enough to justify the eye-watering valuations of edtech.

This needs to change if edtech 3.0 is going to be an improvement on edtech 2.0. Edtech needs to offer much more than just greater reach.

If you dig deeper into the industry dynamics, you will find that every company and entrepreneur thinks of edtech as a consumer technology business. This may be a mischaracterization – education is a service industry, whether it's online or offline. It takes time to show results and create value.

The distinction matters.

Edtech 3.0 will have to start from there. You can't create an edtech company like a fashion brand or an FMCG product, where the engagement is over once you've made the sale. The customer moves on and the company moves on to find the next customer.

In edtech, especially in after-school supplemental education, we are talking about close engagement for a decade. So, the product or the package has to be developed and modified in a way that it can add value to a learner over that long timeframe.

Edtech 3.0 has to be customer-focused in a way that edtech 2.0 has not been. Over the last decade, if you look through the PR narratives, you would realize that edtech businesses were created and positioned to serve the interest of investors and the customers were an afterthought. This has to change.

The good thing is the customer of today is much more aware than they were pre-pandemic. They understand online learning and its pros and cons much better, and a more discerning and demanding customer base could force the next wave of edtech entrepreneurs to recognize that.

So, there's still a big opportunity and the industry could mature and exploit that if entrepreneurs learn from the mistakes of the last 10 years. There has been an erosion of trust, but it can be rebuilt.

I remember making my first online purchase sometime in 2015–16. When I got the delivery, I felt cheated. The product on the website and the real product were nothing similar. I decided online shopping was not for me. I have heard similar stories from many people. But over time, the industry has matured and today, we shop for everything from groceries to laptops online. Edtech will have to go through an analogous process of growing and evolving to deliver what the customer needs.

The truth is that people will never stop looking for an online solution to learning. There are basic challenges that only online modes can solve, like round-the-clock accessibility and reach. There is no way people will stop looking at YouTube tutorials. So online will never go out of fashion. But how can you build a business by offering a satisfactory quality of service and monetizing this need?

That is the real question edtech must now answer.

Demand has seen a crash and the market has bottomed out. So demand can only rise from there. Byju's crash has impacted the formal edtech sector and hurt investors, and this will impede capital flows. But it won't destroy the underlying unsatisfied demand. The market will adjust to try and find solutions in the next few years. Unless, of course, the government decides to adopt brutal regulations similar to China.

That's another cause for concern about the Byju's situation. There are just so many governance and compliance issues with the company. Given that the future of millions of students is at stake, a failure like Byju's might trigger a political backlash that leads to over-regulation.

Another factor is the mechanics of delivery and customer acquisition. The K–12 edtech segment has a high customer acquisition cost (CAC) .

Byju's built its business on push sales with tens of thousands of salespeople and hundreds of millions of dollars spent on advertising and brand-building. Compare that to the word-of-mouth recommendations that build the reputation of the offline tuition centres or, for that matter, turned Raveendran into a phenomenon who could fill stadiums. Word of mouth is not only free, it is priceless.

For any business to be successful, it must have a pull. That is, there has to be something desirable about whatever it is selling. Edtech has to find that magic ingredient, pull, and it has to do so at far lower CAC if it is to evolve to being more than an expensive, loss-making extension of the offline learning model.

The good thing is that technology is evolving every day. Cheaper bandwidth and devices, plus new technologies such as virtual reality, could transform the online experience. Plus there's the promise of artificial intelligence, which could also be game-changing.

The US-based non-profit organization Khan Academy, for example, launched its AI tutor Khanmigo, backed by OpenAI's Chat GPT-4, in July 2023. Khanmigo offers individualized guidance to learners on maths, science and humanities problems; a debate tool that suggests topics such as AI's impact on the job market; and a writing tutor that helps the student craft a story, among other features.

Closer home, Byju's introduced AI to its learning model in June. It is a matter of time before everyone in edtech jumps on the AI bandwagon – how different edtech businesses will use AI, will be a key differentiator, of course.

So, finally, how does edtech deliver an attractive service with 'pull', differentiate itself from offline, do so at acceptable cost and make a profit? There aren't any profitable models around, even though everyone I have spoken with over the last year while working on the book agrees that it must be possible to build a profitable edtech business.

Edtech 3.0 will need to have a full learning experience. It has to offer customized solutions for all needs, and it must keep evolving with the learner for at least three to four years. It has to be completely adaptive. It could be priced high, or it might be a freemium model.

Sales have to be consultative. The business has to adapt rapidly to changes in technology. Ambitions have to be realistic. You can't go to investors and talk about creating a company with $100 billion valuation in 20 years. Break this down into parts. Can you make a company generating revenues of $500 million plus? It is possible. Can you take that company public at $4–$5 billion? Again, yes.

India has more than 250 million students in schools. Is it possible to find 1 million households that can pay $500, or about ₹40,000, for a child's supplemental education? Or 2 million households that pay $250?

There is enough evidence to suggest that parents will pay for the right service if it shows outcomes. Edtech 3.0 will have to be built on that premise. Build it and run it well over the next five to seven years, and the profit and loss account may have $1 billion to show in revenues. At this point, the company can list at a decent valuation – maybe $5–$6 billion and continue to grow.

For all of this to happen, an entrepreneur needs a clear, coherent business plan, around $250 million in funding or more, and realistic targets rather than grandiose ambitions.

The fundamental reason behind the genesis of education technology was the dissatisfaction with the current school infrastructure. But there were always very few options. The opportunity cost of switching off from schools was pretty high. As a result, we witnessed two approaches. One set of entrepreneurs focused on trying to fix schools. The other set thought the problems in schools are not solvable, so let's fix learning through supplemental education. Everyone in the first and the second wave of edtech – from Educomp to

PW – were trying to fix the existing infrastructure one way or another.

'The supply gap is so high and the quality is so poor that most Indian parents end up paying multiple times for education,' says an education expert who has been working in the sector for over two decades.

First, he explains, they pay taxes so the government can open schools. But most of these schools are not up to snuff, so parents pay to get their children enrolled in affordable private schools. But these schools are not good enough either, so parents end up paying a third time, for private tuition. After schooling, depending on what students want to do, parents pay again for test-prep and then for upskilling. Between school and tuition fees, parents are already stretched thin. As a result, only a fraction of those 250 million-plus actually ends up paying for edtech products. With more than 150 million registered users, Byju's, for example, only had 7 million paid subscribers in October 2022. The more realistic current number, according to one person in the know who requested anonymity, is 3-4 million. This is after the company burnt hundreds of millions of dollars in marketing and customer acquisition. It's just not sustainable.

Covid-19 brought the barrier of high opportunity costs for switching off from schools down. It forced people to think outside of the box. Now, there are a number of experiments happening, with technology at the centre of the search for solutions.

One set of entrepreneurs – KaiPod Learning, 21K School, and the like – are working on completely online schools. The idea is to have full-time, borderless virtual schools with in-person learning and support centres to build a community that can support both parents and students. The idea is still in its infancy and is a refined iteration of what existing Indian edtech players are trying to do with blended learning. That said, there is a long way to go.

Changing the mind of a child is a slow process. An edtech business that has the appetite and patience for the long game could become very big and successful.

Most large education businesses, take any Ivy League college, for example, are decades or centuries old. Harvard University is a 400-year-old story. The University of Oxford is almost a millennium old. Think of Pearson and the big publishing houses. Education is a business that slowly gains traction and compounds in value. It's not instant coffee. Any edtech business that wants to be successful in future will have to internalize these and similar insights and review the errors that have occurred in the last 15 years and take care not to commit the same mistakes.

Byju's set the template for edtech 2.0 and also committed most of the egregious missteps and mistakes that led to edtech 2.0 becoming a trainwreck. Can it learn from its mistakes and turn things around?

It seems unlikely but not absolutely impossible that Byju's will manage this. If it does, it will be like a football team that's down 0–2, scoring a winner in injury time.

Notes

Prologue

xv   towards a sustainable long-term year of growth with strong fundamentals: 'Davos 2023 | Byju's 2.0 Will Be Much Better, the Worst Is Behind Us, Says Byju Raveendran', Moneycontrol (2023). https://www.moneycontrol.com/news/business/startup/davos-2023-byjus-2-0-will-be-much-better-the-worst-is-over-for-us-byju-raveendran-9883441.html.

xvi   [T]he arts of business are the arts of bargaining, effrontery, salesmanship, [and] make believe and are directed to the gain of the business man at the cost of the community, at large and in detail: Thorstein Veblen, *Absentee Ownership and Business Enterprise in Recent Times* (1923).

Chapter 1

3   'I remember sitting in a train and predicting its speed by counting the number of electric poles we had crossed in a certain time': John Jong-Hyun Kim and Rachna Tahilyani, 'BYJU'S The Learning App', Harvard Business School (2017).

9   As fate would have it, Mohit became one of his earliest associates: 'Survival, Sustenance, Enterprise: Mrinal Mohit on Building and Scaling a Leading Edtech Brand', Byju's Blog (2021). https://blog.byjus.com/life-at-byjus/people/mrinal-mohit-byjus-building-and-scaling-the-worlds-largest-edtech-brand/.

These are the sources for research and the author's interview/s with Raveendran and others:

— Jayadevan PK, 'The CAT Whisperer', Factor Daily (6 February 2017).

— Anshul Dhamija, 'Ranjan Pai: The Benevolent Investor', *Forbes* (13 July 2017).

— Ann Marie Casanova, 'Cultivating a Love of Learning in K–12', International Finance Corporation (April 2018).

— Thomason Rajan, 'The Unusual Case of BYJU's: Creating One of the World's Most Valued Educational Technology Companies from India', *Indian Journal of Marketing* (April 2022).

— 'Educational Technology Companies from India', *Indian Journal of Marketing* (April 2022).

Chapter 2

22   Yet, unemployment is still hovering around the 8% mark in mid-2023 as I write this: Anup Roy, 'India's Unemployment Rate Falls in July Due to Farm Demand', Bloomberg (2 August 2023). https://www. bloomberg.com/news/articles/2023-08-02/india-s-unemployment-rate-falls-in-july-due-to-farm-demand#xj4y7vzkg.

23   India has one of the world's largest school education systems with around 265 million children: 'Unified District Information System for Education Plus (UDISE+) Report 2021–22', Department of School Education and Literacy, Ministry of Education, Government of India.

23   Around 25% of teachers are absent on any given day:
— Michael Kremer, Nazmul Chaudhury, F. Halsey Rogers, Karthik Muralidharan, Jeffrey Hammer, 'Teacher Absence in India: A Snapshot', *Journal of the European Economic Association* (2005).
— Karthik Muralidharan, Jishnu Das, Alaka Holla and Aakash Mohpal, 'The Fiscal Cost of Weak Governance: Evidence from Teacher Absence in India', *Journal of Public Economics* (2017).

24   In 2018, for example, only one in four students in grade 3 could read grade 2-level text: Annual Status of Education Report (2022).

24   which make up nearly 25% of total schools in India and account for nearly 45% of India's schoolgoing population: 'State of the Sector Report: Private Schools in India', Centre Square Foundation.

25   expected to reach more than $19 billion by 2030, according to Pune-based consultancy Infinium Research: 'Prospects, Trends Analysis, Market Size and Forecasts up to 2030', Infinium Research (April 2023).

25   An estimated 71 million children, nearly one in four school students, attended private tuitions or coaching classes, according to the National Sample Survey 2016:

— Dhamini Ratnam, 'The Tuition Epidemic', *Mint* (12 August 2016). https://www.livemint.com/Leisure/kQl3QWN3rMKoqbjpJp1ScI/ The-tuition-epidemic.html.

— Subodh Verma, '7.1 Cr Students Take Pvt Tuitions: Report', *Times of India* (5 April 2016). http://timesofindia.indiatimes.com/ articleshow/51690266.cms?utm_source=contentofinterest&utm_ medium=text&utm_campaign=cppst.

25 'Edtech in India: A Turning Point', an Omidyar Network India and RedSeer report published in 2020: Namita Dalmia, Sarvesh Kanodia, 'EdTech in India: A Turning Point', Omidyar Network, Redseer (4 May 2020).

27 more than 150 coaching institutes in Kota, catering to around 2,00,000 students aspiring to get into elite engineering: 'Kota Coaching Institutes Address Student Suicide, Focus on Mental Wellbeing', *Business Standard* (31 August 2023). https://www.business-standard.com/education/news/kota-coaching-institutes-address-studentsuicide-focus-on-mental-wellbeing-123083100705_1.html.

27 In 2023, according to Professor Bishnupada Mandal: Pallavi Smart, 'JEE Advanced 2023: IIT Intake Increases, Total 17,385 Seats Available This Year', *Indian Express* (20 June 2023).

27 Every year, tens of thousands of students from Kota's coaching centres clear the JEE Mains exams:
— Aabshar H Quazi, 'Over 39,000 Students from Kota Clear JEE Mains 2017, 48 in Top 100', *Hindustan Times* (28 April 2017).

27 In 2023, four students from Kota made it to the top 10 ranks: IANS, 'IIT JEE Advanced 2023: Four Students from Kota Make It to Top 10 List', *Business Standard* (18 June 2023). https:// www.exchange4media.com/advertising-news/byjus-shah-rukh-khanscript-a-'different-kind-of-love-story'-87169.html.

28 'Any job that doesn't involve a level of creation will be automated,':
— Vishal Krishna, 'Edtech Startup WhiteHat Jr Getting Kids Future-Ready With AI-Based Coding Skills', Yourstory (10 June 2020).

— Rachel John, 'Pushy Indian Parents Now Have a New Goal for Six-Year-Olds – Coding', *The Print* (11 October 2020).

— Rajiv Singh, 'Exclusive: Advertising Body Asks WhiteHat Jr to Pull Down Ads', *Forbes* (27 October 2020).

Chapter 3

35   On Children's Day (14 November) in 2017, Byju's launched one
      of the biggest and most popular ad campaigns of all time: 'BYJU'S
      Math Musical Featuring Shah Rukh Khan', YouTube (13 November
      2017).

35   Our partnership with Shah Rukh Khan will help us increase our
      reach and create a deeper connect across geographies: 'BYJU'S
      & Shah Rukh Khan Script a "Different Kind of Love Story"',
      Exchange4media (4 November 2017). https://www.exchange4media.
      com/advertising-news/byjus-shah-rukh-khan-script-a-'different-
      kind-of-love-story'-87169.html.

35   Children rarely use the word 'Love' and 'Learning' together: Harsh
      Upadhyay, 'Byju's Partners with SRK to Make Children Fall in Love
      With Learning', Entrackr (14 November 2017).

35   'We are proud to be the Indian cricket team sponsor: Saumya
      Tewari, 'Byju's Replaces Oppo as Team India's Official Sponsor:
      BCCI', *Livemint* (25 July 2019). https://www.livemint.com/
      industry/advertising/byju-s-replaces-oppo-as-team-india-s-offical-
      sponsorbcci-1564065067253.html.

36   Here's what Mohit said to Adgully: 'Why Sports Marketing Has
      Worked So Well for BYJU's And New Age Digital Brands', Adgully
      (30 July 2019). https://www.adgully.com/why-sports-marketing-
      has-worked-so-well-for-byju-s-new-age-digital-brands-87330.
      html.

42   they show them Raveendran's introduction to geometry video: 'Class
      6–10 – An Introduction to Geometry | Learn with Byju's', YouTube
      (4 August 2015).

44   Finally, the salesperson would ask for PAN and Aadhaar numbers
      and bank details: Pradip K. Saha, 'The Great Indian Edtech Refunds
      Scam', The Morning Context (19 July 2021).

48   I found out that the company was paying EMIs on behalf of the
      customer: Pradip K. Saha, 'At Byju's, A Loan Crisis and No Sign
      of Funding', The Morning Context (20 March 2023). https://
      themorningcontext.com/internet/at-byjus-a-loan-crisis-and-no-
      sign-of-funding.

49   Remember the 100% FLDG agreement between Byju's and the
      lenders?:
      — Vishwanath Nair, 'RBI Allows 5% Default Loss Cover for Bank-
      Fintech Deals', BQ Prime (8 June 2023).

— Pratik Bhakta, 'Byju's Crisis Plays Up Digital Lenders' Asset Quality Problem', *The Economic Times* (26 June 2023).

Chapter 4

54   **Students needed on-demand tutoring from qualified teachers:** Sue Shellenbarger, 'The Invasion of the Online Tutors', *The Wall Street Journal* (12 November 2013). https://www.wsj.com/articles/the-invasion-of-the-online-tutors-1384301976.

55   **in 2007, less than two years into the business, TutorVista acquired Edurite Technologies:** Ruchika Sharma, '"We Are Looking at Acquisitions": K. Ganesh', VCCircle (22 July 2009). https://www.vccircle.com/we-are-looking-acquisitions-k-ganesh.

55   **It first bought a minority stake and eventually acquired TutorVista for about $150 million:** Prashant K. Nanda, 'Pearson Acquires Whole of TutorVista', *Mint* (24 February 2013). https://www.livemint.com/Companies/LkipTPnsANIBwtrLBJOnHJ/Pearson-acquires-whole-of-TutorVista.html.

56   **in 2017, Pearson sold the business to Byju's for a paltry $3 million:** Sayan Chakraborty, 'Byju's Buys Pearson's TutorVista, Edurite in Push for Global Expansion', *Mint* (3 July 2017). https://www.livemint.com/Companies/VtOJY1jBZSOrtBvyLzsrhI/Byjus-acquires-TutorVista-Eduvista-in-push-for-global-expa.html.

56   **Educomp Solutions, started by IIM Ahmedabad alumnus Shantanu Prakash in 1994:** Manoj Gairola, 'How Educomp May Have Subverted the Spirit of India's Insolvency and Bankruptcy Process', The Wire (3 April 2018). https://thewire.in/business/how-educomp-may-have-subverted-the-spirit-of-indias-insolvency-and-bankruptcy-process.

56   **by 2012 its revenues touched ₹1,000 crore:** M. Saraswathy, 'A Look at the Rise and Downfall of Ed-tech Messiah Shantanu Prakash', Moneycontrol (12 February 2020). https://www.moneycontrol.com/news/business/companies/a-look-at-the-rise-and-downfall-of-ed-tech-messiah-shantanu-prakash-4936861.html.

57   **It filed for bankruptcy in 2017:** Manoj Gairola, 'How Educomp May Have Subverted the Spirit of India's Insolvency and Bankruptcy Process', The Wire (3 April 2018). https://thewire.in/business/how-educomp-may-have-subverted the-spirit-of-indias-insolvency-and-bankruptcy-process.

58   Flipkart raised $200 million from marquee investors like Tiger
      Global and Accel: 'Flipkart Raises $200 Million from Investors',
      NDTV Profit (10 July 2013). https://www.ndtv.com/business/
      flipkart-raises-200-million-from-investors-324283.

58   In 2015, venture capitalists doubled the amount they had pumped
      into Indian start-ups: 'Investment in an Indian Start-up Every
      8 Hours', *Business Standard* (30 December 2015). https://www.
      business-standard.com/article/companies/investment-in-an-indian-
      start-up-every-8-hours-115122900850_1.html.

59   2015 saw the emergence of over 1,000 start-ups in edtech: Ashish
      Gupta, 'The Edtech Story #1: The Edtech Landscape: A Brief
      Overview', Nasscom (6 August 2020). https://community.nasscom.
      in/communities/talent/edtech/the-edtech-story-1-the-edtech-
      landscape-a-brief-overview.html.

59   Internet penetration in India stood at around 30% in 2015: Telecom
      Regulatory Authority of India Annual Report 2014–15.

59   It was a lot better than 7.5% in 2010: Telecom Regulatory Authority
      of India Recommendations on National Broadband Plan (8
      December 2010).

59   a large mobile phone user base will be one big reason for the adoption
      of education technology in the future: Joshua Kim, '3 Reasons
      Why India Will Lead EdTech in the 21st Century', *Forbes* (10
      August 2012). https://www.forbesindia.com/article/tuck-school-
      of-business/3-reasons-why-india-will-lead-edtech-in-the-21st-
      century/33456/1.

60   Reliance Jio launched in late 2016: 'Reliance Jio Launched in Late
      2016', *The Indian Express* (1 September 2016). https://indianexpress.
      com/article/technology/mobile-tabs/reliance-jio-4g-service-
      launch-highlights-tariff-data-voice-calls-3007532/.

60   the Telecom Regulatory Authority of India said that the cost of
      mobile data had fallen by about 95%: 'Mobile Data Cost Dived 95%
      Post-Jio, Says TRAI', *The New Indian Express* (22 August 2019).
      https://www.newindianexpress.com/business/2019/aug/22/mobile-
      data-cost-dived-95-post-jio-says-trai-2022561.html.

61   Another 30 million Indians use fixed broadband via fibre: Telecom
      Regulatory Authority of India Press Release No.77/2023 (24 August
      2023). https://www.trai.gov.in/sites/default/files/PR_No.77of2023.
      pdf.

63   'We have more data on our food delivery guys than we have on
      our tuition teachers, or coaching classes,': Pradip K. Saha, Zishaan
      Hayath, 'Riding the Hockey-Stick Curve', The Morning Context (25
      September 2020). https://themorningcontext.com/internet/zishaan-
      hayath-riding-the-hockey-stick-curve.

63   Coaching classes are discriminatory: Pradip K. Saha, Zishaan
      Hayath, 'Riding the Hockey-Stick Curve', The Morning Context (25
      September 2020). https://themorningcontext.com/internet/zishaan-
      hayath-riding-the-hockey-stick-curve.

64   The gross enrolment ratio in India is about 27% for colleges: Pradip
      K. Saha, 'Opportunity in Online Higher Ed Is So Big No One Player
      Can Do It Themselves', The Morning Context (9 May 2023). https://
      themorningcontext.com/internet/opportunity-in-online-higher-ed-
      is-so-big-no-one-player-can-do-it-themselves.

65   few centres except the marquee ones make serious money: Pradip
      K. Saha, 'Why Are Edtech Firms Opening Coaching Centres?', The
      Morning Context (17 June 2022). https://themorningcontext.com/
      internet/why-are-edtech-firms-opening-coaching-centres.

Chapter 5

67   Bloomberg had just reported that Byju's had acquired Aakash
      for around $1 billion: Saritha Rai, 'Byju's to Pay $1 Billion for
      Blackstone-Backed India Tutor', Bloomberg (12 January 2021).
      https://www.bloomberg.com/news/articles/2021-01-12/byju-s-
      said-to-pay-1-billion-for-blackstone-backed-india-tutor.

69   Blackstone Group's investment in the offline coaching company,
      in October 2019, valued it at just $500 million: Ridhima Saxena,
      'Blackstone Invests in Test Prep Firm Aakash', Mint (30 October
      2019). https://www.livemint.com/companies/news/blackstone-
      buys-37-5-stake-in-aakash-educational-services-11572442785208.
      html.

71   According to a UNESCO report, the pandemic affected over 1.5
      billion students globally: 'Education: From School Closure to
      Recovery', UNESCO. https://en.unesco.org/themes/education-
      emergencies/coronavirus-school-closures.

72   In India, Amit Khare, secretary in India's Ministry of Human
      Resource Development: 'Amit Khare's Letter COVID-19: STAY
      SAFE Digital Learning Initiatives of Ministry of HRD', D.O. No.

Secy(HE)/MHRD/2020 (20 March 2020). https://www.mohfw.gov. in/pdf/Covid19.pdf.

72 **Byju's, with over 42 million users and a valuation north of $8 billion at the time, announced on 11 March:** Pradip K. Saha, 'Edtech Firms Hope for a New Normal', The Morning Context (2 April 2020). https://themorningcontext.com/internet/edtech-firms-hope-for-a-new-normal.

72 **'This is an opportunity for us to generate trials,':** Pradip K. Saha, 'Edtech Firms Hope for a New Normal', The Morning Context (2 April 2020). https://themorningcontext.com/internet/edtech-firms-hope-for-a-new-normal.

73 **Byju's reported a 60% increase in the number of students:** Sanchita Dash, 'Byju's Sees a 60 per cent Increase in New Students after Making Its App Free for All', *Business Insider* (18 March 2020). https://www.businessinsider.in/byjus-sees-a-60-increase-in-new-students-after-making-its-app-free-for-all/articleshow/74692509. cms.

73 **It introduced the National Education Policy, 2020 on 29 July, the first such policy in 34 years:** 'National Education Policy 2020 Announced', PIB (29 July 2020). https://pib.gov.in/PressReleasePage. aspx?PRID=1642061#:~:text=The%20Union%20Cabinet%20 chaired%20by,Education%20(NPE)%2C1986.

73 **Section 23 of the policy is dedicated to the use of technology and its integration:** 'National Education Policy 2020', Ministry of Human Resource Development. https://www.education.gov.in/sites/upload_files/mhrd/files/NEP_Final_English_0.pdf.

74 **According to an April 2021 Ernst & Young report on online learning platforms in India:** 'Market Roundup | Online Learning Platforms in India Edition', EY (April 2021). https://assets.ey.com/content/dam/ey-sites/ey-com/en_in/topics/covid-19/eyp-online-learning-platforms-09-april-2021.pdf?download.

75 **PE/VC investment in edtech between 2020 and 2022 accounted for more than 70% of the total investment in the sector:** 'PE/VC Agenda India Trend Book 2023', EY (2023). https://assets.ey.com/content/dam/ey-sites/ey-com/en_in/topics/private-equity/2023/ey-pe-vc-annual-trend-book-2023.pdf.

76 **In 2021, the Chinese government took a landmark decision:** 'China Bans For-Profit School Tutoring in Sweeping Overhaul', Bloomberg (24 July 2021). https://www.bloomberg.com/news/

articles/2021-07-24/china-bans-school-curriculum-tutoring-firms-from-going-public.

76   **China and India have the world's first and second largest education system:**
— Nirmala Rao, Kai-Ming Cheng and Kirti Narain, 'Primary Schooling in China and India: Understanding How Socio-Contextual Factors Moderate the Role of the State', *International Review of Education* (March 2003).
— Mark Bray, 'Comparative Education: Continuing Traditions, New Challenges, and New Paradigms', *International Review of Education* (January 2003).

77   **In cities like Beijing, Shanghai, Guangzhou and Shenzhen, 70% of the students in kindergarten through grade 12 receive after-school tutoring:** Chong Koh Ping and Quentin Webb, 'China's Tutoring Restraint Slams Stocks', *The Wall Street Journal* (26 July 2021). https://www.wsj.com/articles/chinas-tutoring-rules-slam-education-stocks-11627276804.

77   **Calling out the industry's 'disorderly development':** Yujie Xuein and Tracy Quin, 'China Two Sessions: Tightened Regulation of "Chaotic" K–12 Off-Campus Education Market May Spoil Big Tech's Expansion Plans', *South China Morning Post* (11 March 2021). https://www.scmp.com/tech/policy/article/3125051/china-two-sessions-2021-tightened-regulation-chaotic-k-12-campus.

77   **In announcing the rules, China's education ministry said:** Ryan McMorrow, Sun Yu, Tabby Kinder, Thomas Hale, 'China's Education Sector Crackdown Hits Foreign Investors', *Financial Times* (26 July 2021). https://www.ft.com/content/dfae3282-e14e-4fea-aa5f-c2e914444fb8.

77   **China, prior to the policy change was home to 8 out of the world's 28 edtech unicorns:** Kritti Bhalla, 'The Chinese Government Believes Online Education Is Bad for Students, Parents and The Society', *Business Insider India* (26 July 2021). https://www.businessinsider.in/education/news/the-chinese-government-believes-online-education-is-bad-for-students-parents-and-the-society/articleshow/84752031.cms.

78   **The PRC's edtech industry attracted $10 billion in 2020:**
—Rohan D'Souza, 'What Lies Behind China's Crackdown on Ed-Tech Companies', *The Indian Express* (9 September 2021). https://indianexpress.com/article/opinion/columns/china-crackdown-ed-tech-companies-7495277/.

—Shelly Xu, 'How China's Edtech Market Is Booming in the "Stay At Home Era"', The Org (15 February 2023). https://theorg. com/iterate/how-chinas-edtech-market-is-booming-in-the-stay-at-home-era.

78 Apart from the China angle, there was also FOMO on two levels: Pradip K. Saha, 'How Did Indian VCs Get Their Edtech Hypothesis So Wrong?', The Morning Context (10 October 2023). https:// themorningcontext.com/internet/how-did-indian-vcs-get-their-edtech-hypothesis-so-wrong.

79 Byju's valuation grew nearly threefold from $8 billion in March 2020: Manish Singh, 'Indian Education Startup Byju's Raises $200M from General Atlantic', TechCrunch (7 February 2020). https://techcrunch. com/2020/02/07/indian-education-startup-byjus-raises-200m-from-general-atlantic/.

79 to $22 billion in March 2022: Harsh Upadhyay, 'Byju's Raises $800 Mn at $22 Bn Valuation; Founder Infuses $400 Mn', Entrackr (11 March 2022). https://entrackr.com/2022/03/byjus-raises-800-mn-at-22-bn-valuation-founder-infuses-400-mn/.

81 He knew or suspected growth in the home market would taper soon: Udayan Mukherjee, 'Udayan Mukherjee in Conversation with Byju Raveendran', Business Today (28 August 2021).

82 Zomato, for example, entered the US market in 2015: Catherine Shu, 'Restaurant Discovery Site Zomato Buys IAC's Urbanspoon, Enters the U.S.', TechCrunch (12 January 2015) https://techcrunch. com/2015/01/12/restaurant-discovery-site-zomato-buys-iacs-urbanspoon-enters-the-u-s-market/.

82 tried different things and, eventually, shut down the US business just before it went public in 2021: Payal Ganguly, 'Zomato to Cease US Ops, Sharpen Focus on India Biz', Mint (20 August 2021). https://www.livemint.com/companies/news/zomato-to-cease-us-operations-sharpen-focus-on-india-11629460236545.html.

82 It took barely a year for hotel owners to find out that OYO's business is all bait and switch: Ashish K. Mishra, 'OYO's International Ambitions Lie In Tatters', The Morning Context (23 October 2020). https://themorningcontext.com/business/oyos-international-ambitions-lie-in-tatters.

82 the company would move fast and invest $1 billion in the next three years in the US: 'Udayan Mukherjee in Conversation With

Byju Raveendran', *Business Today* (28 August 2021). https://www.businesstoday.in/news-reel/video/udayan-mukherjee-in-conversation-with-byju-raveendran-305394-2021-08-28.

82 **But Raveendran was doubling down:** Udayan Mukherjee, 'Udayan Mukherjee in Conversation with Byju Raveendran', *Business Today* (28 August 2021).

82 **So, he raised $1.2 billion via a term loan B arrangement in the US in November 2021:** Saritha Rai, 'Blackstone, GIC Help Byju's Boost Loan Target to $1 Billion', Bloomberg (8 November 2021). https://www.bloomberg.com/news/articles/2021-11-08/blackstone-gic-help-byju-s-to-boost-loan-target-to-1-2-billion.

83 **Raveendran had been talking about crossing ₹10,000 crore in revenue:** Manish Singh, 'Indian Decacorn Byju's CEO Talks about Future Acquisitions, Coronavirus and International Expansion', *TechCrunch* (15 September 2020).

Chapter 6

85 'It emanates from the incessant pressure of targets,' says Pratik Makhija: Pradip K. Saha, 'Under Pressure, Byju's Sales Machinery is Showing Cracks', The Morning Context (29 August 2022).

86 'We have the best people. In fact, our competitors hire salespeople from us.': Pradip K. Saha, 'How Byju's Catches Parents', The Morning Context (11 March 2020).

91 the goal for a salesperson was to bring ₹1.5 lakh in sales a week: Pradip K. Saha, 'Under Pressure, Byju's Sales Machinery Is Showing Cracks', The Morning Context (29 August 2022). https://themorningcontext.com/internet/under-pressure-byjus-sales-machinery-is-showingcracks.

101 Unit economics is wonky at Byju's: Pradip K. Saha, 'Under Pressure, Byju's Sales Machinery Is Showing Cracks', The Morning Context (29 August 2022).

103 The impact – as many observers have pointed out – has been even worse than apparent: Ashish K. Mishra and Pradip K. Saha, 'Byju's Numbers Continue to Confound', The Morning Context (6 September 2021).

Chapter 7

106 **the company announced that it would launch 500 tuition centres across 200 cities:** 'BYJU'S Launches "BYJU'S Tuition Centre" across India, Combining the Best of Offline and Online Learning Experiences', Byju's Blog (17 February 2022).

106 **Mohit told YourStory that the company was not 'going from digital to offline:** Apurva P, 'Byju's Makes Strong Offline Push with Plan to Launch 500 Tuition Centres In 2022', YourStory (17 February 2022). https://yourstory.com/socialstory/2022/02/byjus-launches-byjus-tuition-centre-offline-centres.

108 **Lido Learning shut down operations and asked nearly 1,200 employees to resign:** Pradip K. Saha, 'The Real Tragedy of Lido Learning's Failure', The Morning Context (26 February 2022). https://themorningcontext.com/internet/the-real-tragedy-of-lido-learnings-failure.

109 **In September 2022 when Lido Learning filed for bankruptcy:** 'Lido Learning Files for Bankruptcy', *The Hindu BusinessLine* (8 September 2022). https://www.thehindubusinessline.com/companies/lido-learning-files-for-bankruptcy/article65866119.ece.

111 **There was a bloodbath on the Nasdaq:** 'Stock Market News for Jan 24, 2022', Nasdaq (24 January 2022). https://www.nasdaq.com/articles/stock-market-news-for-jan-24-2022.

111 **VC funds started warning their portfolio companies:** Mark Di Stefano, Kate Clark and Nick Wingfield, 'Sequoia Warns Founders of "Crucible Moment," Advises How to "Avoid the Death Spiral"', The Information (24 May 2022).

111 **The Menlo Park, California, headquartered Sequoia Capital:** Mark Di Stefano, Kate Clark and Nick Wingfield, 'Sequoia Warns Founders of "Crucible Moment," Advises How to "Avoid the Death Spiral"', The Information (24 May 2022). https://www.theinformation.com/articles/sequoia-warns-founders-of-crucible-moment-advises-how-to-avoid-the-death-spiral.

112 **Then the company acquired Aakash Education and Gradeup to get into test-prep:**
— Pradip K. Saha, 'Why "Offline" Aakash Will Give Byju's the Edtech Edge', The Morning Context (15 January 2021). https://themorningcontext.com/internet/why-offline-aakash-will-give-byjus-the-edtech-edge.
— Jai Vardhan and Harsh Upadhyay, 'Exclusive: Byju's in Talks

to Acquire Great Learning and Gradeup for $400 Mn', Entrackr (29 April 2021). https://entrackr.com/2021/04/exclusive-byjus-to-acquire-great-learning-and-gradeup-for-400-mn/.

113 **In India, the education ministry's National Achievement Survey (NAS) 2021:** National Achievement Survey 2021. https://nas.gov.in/report-card/nas-2021.

114 **we faced roadblocks in growing the original model:** Harsh Upadhyay, 'Exclusive: Alpha Wave-Backed Edtech Startup Udayy Shuts Down', Entrackr (1 June 2022). https://entrackr.com/2022/06/exclusive-alpha-wave-backed-edtech-startup-udayy-shuts-down/.

115 **'. . . we never thought of doing K–12. Somewhere down the journey, people started comparing us with Byju's':** Pradip K. Saha, "Our K–12 business Was Driven Purely by FOMO": Gaurav Munjal, The Morning Context (4 April 2022).

Chapter 8

119 **Byju's plan to explore a public listing in the US through a special purpose acquisition company (SPAC):** Saritha Rai, Gillian Tan and Anto Antony, 'India's Most Valuable Startup Byju's in Talks to Go Public via SPAC Deal: Sources', Bloomberg (16 December 2021). https://www.bloomberg.com/news/articles/2021-12-16/byju-s-is-said-in-talks-to-go-public-through-churchill-spac-deal.

119 **Byju's was in talks with Michael Dell's MSD Acquisition Corp. and Altimeter Capital Management for a possible SPAC merger:** Saritha Rai, Gillian Tan and Anto Antony, 'India's Most Valuable Startup Byju's in Talks to Go Public via SPAC Deal: Sources', Bloomberg (16 December 2021). https://www.bloomberg.com/news/articles/2021-12-16/byju-s-is-said-in-talks-to-go-public-through-churchill-spac-deal.

122 **In March 2022, the Indian government mothballed its previous policy directive to allow Indian companies to list overseas:** Aftab Ahmed, Aditi Shah and Aditya Kalra, 'Exclusive India Mothballs Plan to Let Local Firms List Overseas: Sources', Reuters (24 March 2022). https://www.reuters.com/world/india/exclusive-india-mothballs-plan-let-local-firms-list-overseas-sources-2022-03-23/.

122 **the SPAC plan was off because of the crash in global markets:** Ashish K. Mishra and Pradip K. Saha, 'Byju's SPAC Plan Looks Shaky', The Morning Context (31 January 2022).

124 According to data from SPACInsider: 'IPO Transactions by Year', SPACInsider. https://www.spacinsider.com/data/stats.

126 Byju's announced in March 2022 that it had raised $800 million from Sumeru Ventures:
— Team Storyweavers, 'Byju Raveendran Invests $400 Million in BYJU'S as Part of $800-Million Fundraise', Byju's Blog (17 March 2022).
— Pradip K. Saha, 'The Fake Investment That Connects Byju's and Sri Sri Ravi Shankar', The Morning Context (4 July 2022).
— Yatti Soni, 'BYJU'S Raises $800 M Funding Round At a Valuation Of $22 billion, *The Hindu BusinessLine* (11 March 2022). https://www.thehindubusinessline.com/companies/byjus-raises-800-m-funding-round-at-a-valuation-of-22-billion/article65214631.ece.

126 So I dug deeper for whatever information was available about Sumeru Ventures: Pradip K. Saha, 'The Fake Investment That Connects Byju's and Sri Sri Ravi Shankar', The Morning Context (4 July 2022). https://themorningcontext.com/internet/the-fake-investment-that-connects-byjus-and-sri-sri-ravi-shankar.

127 There were two people managing the fund – Jatin Chaurasia and Saumen Chakraborty: Pradip K. Saha, 'The Truth about Sumeru Ventures', The Morning Context (25 July 2022).

128 shows Chakraborty is associated with multiple companies as a director: Pradip K. Saha, 'The Truth About Sumeru Ventures', The Morning Context (25 July 2022). https://themorningcontext.com/internet/the-truth-about-sumeru-ventures.

129 Axis Bank alleged 'cheating and forgery' by Intellisys Technologies and Research to the tune of ₹21.75 crore: https://bond.bseindia.com/PPMFiles/2021/DEC/PPM/28/4918.pdf.

131 We went ahead and published the story: Pradip K. Saha, 'The Fake Investment That Connects Byju's And Sri Sri Ravi Shankar', The Morning Context (4 July 2022). https://themorningcontext.com/internet/the-fake-investment-that-connects-byjus-and-sri-sri-ravi-shankar.

132 a quick look at the domain name system (DNS) entries for Sumeru Ventures and Sumeru Inc., which showed the websites were still being managed by Namit Behl:
— DNS entry for Sumeru Ventures: https://www.whatsmydns.net/#SOA/sumeruventure.com.

— DNS entry for Sumeru Inc.: https://www.whatsmydns.net/#SOA/ sumeru.us.

134 **We learnt money from Oxshott Capital Partners:** Pradip K. Saha, 'Oxshott's Fake Investment in Byju's and a Missing Rs 1,200 Crore', The Morning Context (11 July 2022).

136 **Raveendran has since accepted in interviews:** Deepsekhar Choudhury, Chandra R Srikanth and Nikhil Patwardhan, '"If This Didn't Break Us, Nothing Will": Byju Raveendran Opens Up About Troubles of Last Six Months', Moneycontrol (14 September 2022).

Chapter 9

139 **the company released selected numbers to select journalists:** Ashish K. Mishra and Pradip K. Saha, 'Byju's 2020-21 Financials Show It's a House of Cards', The Morning Context (15 September 2022).

139 **The numbers, as expected, were disastrous:** Ashish K. Mishra and K. Saha, 'Byju's 2020-21 Financials Show It's a House of Cards', The Morning Context (15 September 2022). https://themorningcontext. com/internet/byjus-2020-21-financials-show-its-a-house-of-cards.

141 **Deloitte, Byju's auditor, finally ran out of patience with the company's fuzzy accounting practices:** Ashish K. Mishra and Pradip K. Saha, 'Byju's Numbers Continue to Confound', The Morning Context (6 September 2021).

143 **Revenues from transfer of products to certain customers made under deferred payment terms and totalling to Rs 1,156.27 crore:** Auditor's note, Page 223, Think & Learn Pvt. Ltd Consolidated Financial Statements for period 1 April 2020 to 31 March 2021.

144 **In the current year, the Parent has retrospectively adjusted the following:** Auditor's note, Page 45, Think & Learn Pvt. Ltd Consolidated Financial Statements for period 1 April 2020 to 31 March 2021.

145/ **(i) Revenue is recognised upon transfer of control of promised**
146 **products or services to customers . . .**

(ii) The group in its normal course of business sells educational content to its customers via SD cards . . .

(iii) Sale of Edutech products to customers primarily involves 3 modes of settlement by customers . . .

(iv) In cases where the customer takes a loan from the Loan partners . . .

(v) In cases where the customers are provided deferred payment terms by the Parent . . .:
— Auditor's note, Pages 34–35, Think & Learn Pvt. Ltd Consolidated Financial Statements for period 1 April 2020 to 31 March 2021.

150 Revenues from sale of educational content to customers based in the Gulf Cooperation Council (GCC) countries: Auditor's note, Page 223, Think & Learn Pvt. Ltd Consolidated Financial Statements for period 1 April 2020 to 31 March 2021.

151 (ii) Sale to retail customers in the Gulf Cooperation Council (GCC) countries . . .: Auditor's note, Page 33, Think & Learn Pvt. Ltd Consolidated Financial Statements for period 1 April 2020 to 31 March 2021.

152 sceptical about the Middle East revenues: Pradip K. Saha, 'With 2U Deal Off, Byju's Ambitions Suffer a Setback', The Morning Context (27 September).

153 The best year, said this person, was 2017–18: Pradip K. Saha, 'With 2U Deal Off, Byju's Ambitions Suffer a Setback', The Morning Context (27 September 2022). https://themorningcontext.com/internet/with-2u-deal-off-byjus-ambitions-suffer-a-setback.

153 Here's what the company said in its response: Pradip K. Saha, 'With 2U Deal Off, Byju's Ambitions Suffer a Setback', The Morning Context (27 September 2022). https://themorningcontext.com/internet/with-2u-deal-off-byjus-ambitions-suffer-a-setback.

154 In his post-earnings interview with Moneycontrol: Deepsekhar Choudhury, Chandra R Srikanth and Nikhil Patwardhan, "If This Didn't Break Us, Nothing Will": Byju Raveendran Opens Up about Troubles of Last Six Months', Moneycontrol (14 September 2022). https://www.moneycontrol.com/news/interview/byju-raveendran-opens-up-about-troubles-of-last-6-months-says-if-this-didnt-break-us-nothing-will-9179191.html.

155 given that the investments from Sumeru Ventures and Oxshott Capital: Deepsekhar Choudhury, Chandra R. Srikanth and Nikhil Patwardhan, "If This Didn't Break Us, Nothing Will": Byju Raveendran Opens Up about Troubles of Last Six Months', Moneycontrol (14 September 2022).

155 'Now, the $300 million from Sumeru and Oxshott is not coming, but that is not our mistake.': Deepsekhar Choudhury, Chandra R. Srikanth and Nikhil Patwardhan, "If This Didn't Break Us, Nothing Will": Byju Raveendran Opens Up about Troubles of

Last Six Months', Moneycontrol (14 September 2022). https://
www.moneycontrol.com/news/interview/byju-raveendran-opens-
up-about-troubles-of-last-6-months-says-if-this-didnt-break-us-
nothing-will-9179191.html.

156 **In the second week of October, Gokulnath and Mohit issued
separate statements:**
— Reuters, 'Byju's Aims for Profitability by March 2023, Plans to
Fire 2,500 People, *Hindustan Times* (12 October 2022). https://
www.hindustantimes.com/business/byjus-aims-for-profitability-by-
march-2023-plans-to-fire-2-500-people-101665580370427.html.
— PTI, 'To Become Profitable, Byju's to Lay Off 2,500 Employees
in Next Six Months', NDTV (12 October 2022). https://www.ndtv.
com/india-news/byjus-to-lay-off-2-500-employees-in-next-six-
months-to-become-profitable-3425572.

156 **Gokulnath said the jobs cuts would happen across:** PTI, 'To Become
Profitable, Byju's to Lay Off 2,500 Employees in Next Six Months',
NDTV (12 October 2022). https://www.ndtv.com/india-news/
byjus-to-lay-off-2-500-employees-in-next-six-months-to-become-
profitable-3425572.

160 **the company was firing between 12,000 and 15,000 people:** Pradip
K. Saha, 'Byju's to Lay Off Nearly 12,000, a Quarter of Its Staff', The
Morning Context (27 October 2022).

162 **We published the story the next morning:** Pradip K. Saha, 'Byju's to
Lay Off Nearly 12,000, a Quarter of Its Staff', The Morning Context
(27 October 2022). https://themorningcontext.com/internet/byjus-
to-lay-off-nearly-12000-a-quarter-of-its-staff.

164 **the company was facing a severe cash crunch:** Ashish K. Mishra
and Pradip K. Saha, 'Byju's Promoters Have Sold Shares Worth
Millions of Dollars', The Morning Context (15 November 2022).
https://themorningcontext.com/internet/byjus-promoters-have-
sold-shares-worth-millions-of-dollars.

164 **Byju Raveendran, his brother Riju Ravindran and Byju's wife, Divya
Gokulnath – had sold 25% of their total holdings:**
— Ashish K. Mishra and Pradip K. Saha, 'Byju's Promoters Have
Sold Shares Worth Millions of Dollars', The Morning Context (15
November 2022).
— Ujjaini Dutta and Diti Pujara, 'Byju's Promoters Sold Shares
Worth $408.53 Mn since 2015: Privatecircle Research', The Morning
Context (4 July 2023).

165 the promoters sold shares worth around $408.53 million in 40
     secondary transactions since 2015: Ujjaini Dutta and Diti Pujara,
     'Byju's Promoters Sold Shares Worth $408.53 Mn Since 2015:
     PrivateCircle Research', The Morning Context (4 July 2023). https://
     themorningcontext.com/yesterday/the-byjus-sold-shares-worth-
     over-400-mn-over-8-years.

166 said the fair value of its 9.67% stake in Byju's was $578 million: Pradip
     K. Saha, 'Prosus Pegs Byju's Valuation at $6 Billion', The Morning
     Context (23 November 2022). https://themorningcontext.com/
     internet/prosus-pegs-byjus-valuation-at-6-billion-the-morning-
     context.

Chapter 10

168 hadn't paid several of its vendors for months: Pradip K. Saha, 'Byju's
     Is in the Throes of a Working Capital Crisis', The Morning Context
     (16 December 2022). https://themorningcontext.com/internet/
     byjus-is-in-the-throes-of-a-working-capital-crisis.

168 In the eight months to October 2022, cumulative dues to vendors
     had crossed ₹90 crore: Pradip K. Saha, 'Byju's Is in the Throes of a
     Working Capital Crisis', The Morning Context (16 December 2022).
     https://themorningcontext.com/internet/byjus-is-in-the-throes-
     ofa-working-capital-crisis.

169 Individual tax statements showed that Byju's last deposited TDS
     for April 2022: Pradip K. Saha, 'Byju's Is in the Throes of a Working
     Capital Crisis', The Morning Context (16 December 2022). https://
     themorningcontext.com/internet/byjus-is-in-the-throes-of-a-
     working-capital-crisis.

169 Around February 2023, we discovered that Byju's was paying EMIs
     on behalf of customers: Pradip K. Saha, 'At Byju's, a Loan Crisis
     and No Sign of Funding', The Morning Context (20 March 2023).
     https://themorningcontext.com/internet/at-byjus-a-loan-crisis-
     andno-sign-of-funding.

171 Then the company breached a covenant of the credit agreement:
     Pradip K. Saha, 'Lawsuit Filed by Byju's Lenders Details a String
     of Broken Promises', The Morning Context (20 June 2023). https://
     themorningcontext.com/internet/lawsuit-filed-by-byjus-lenders-
     details-a-string-of-broken-promises.

171 **On 30 June 2023, LIBOR was replaced by the Secured Overnight Financing Rate:** Joe Rennison, 'The End of LIBOR Is (Finally) Here', *The New York Times* (30 June 2023). https://www.nytimes.com/2023/06/30/business/end-of-libor.html.

171 **In May, lenders sued Byju's Alpha:** Steven Church and Jef Feeley, 'Byju's Alpha Accused of Hiding $500 Million from Lenders', Bloomberg (19 May 2023). https://www.bloomberg.com/news/articles/2023-05-18/byju-s-alpha-hid-500-million-from-lenderslawyer-tells-judge.

172 **The company agreed to repay the loan in 'quarterly instalments of 0.25% of the aggregate principal':** GLAS Trust Company vs Riju Ravindran Byju's Alpha Inc., and Tangible Play Inc., case number, 2023-0488, Delaware Chancery Court (Wilmington).

172 **43. Article 5 of the Credit Agreement enumerates . . .**
44. Pursuant to Section 5.1(b), Think and Learn further . . .
47. Furthermore, pursuant to Section 5.9(c) of the Credit . . .
— GLAS Trust Company vs Riju Ravindran Byju's Alpha Inc., and Tangible Play Inc., case number, 2023-0488, Delaware Chancery Court (Wilmington)

176 **A raid by the Enforcement Directorate on Byju's in India spooked the lenders further:** GLAS Trust Company vs Riju Ravindran Byju's Alpha Inc., and Tangible Play Inc., case number, 2023-0488, Delaware Chancery Court (Wilmington).

176 **A PTI report said the action was taken on the basis of 'various complaints':** PTI, 'ED Conducts Searches against BYJU's CEO Raveendran, Says He Never Appeared for Questioning', *Outlook Start-Up* (29 April 2023). https://startup.outlookindia.com/sector/ed-tech/ed-conducts-searches-against-byju-s-ceo-raveendran-says-he-never-appeared-for-questioning-news-8294#:~:text=Press%20Trust%20Of%20India&text=It%20said%20the%20action%20was,company%2C%20Think%20%26%20Learn%20Pvt.

177 **On 6 June, the company filed a counter complaint against lenders in the New York Supreme Court:**
— Byju's Pte. Ltd vs GLAS Trust Company, New York Supreme Court.
— Pradip K. Saha, 'How Did Byju's Get in Trouble with the Term Loan B?', The Morning Context (9 June 2023). https://themorningcontext.com/internet/how-did-byjus-get-in-trouble-with-the-term-loan-b.

177 It also refused to pay $40 million in interest: Rachel Butt and Reshmi Basu, 'High-Flying Indian Startup Byju's Skips Payment on Dollar Loan', Bloomberg (6 June 2023).

180 In an interview with *Business Today*'s Udayan Mukherjee in August 2021, he admitted as much: 'Udayan Mukherjee in conversation with Byju Raveendran', *Business Today* (28 August 2021). https://www.businesstoday.in/news-reel/video/udayan-mukherjee-in-conversation-with-byju-raveendran-305394-2021-08-28.

181 the online learning vertical was estimated to be logging a monthly run rate of around ₹150 crore: Pradip K. Saha, 'Davidson Kempner Accuses Byju's of Financial Misconduct, Takes Control of Aakash', The Morning Context (31 July 2023). https://themorningcontext.com/internet/davidson-kempner-accuses-byjus-of-financial-misconduct-takes-control-of-aakash.

182 Almost two years on, the tuition centre business is in tatters: Pradip K. Saha, 'Byju's Tuitions Business Is Falling Apart', The Morning Context (19 July 2023). https://themorningcontext.com/internet/byjus-tuitions-business-is-falling-apart.

184 At the end of July 2023, Byju's had 302 tuition centres, all bleeding money: Pradip K. Saha, 'Byju's Tuitions Business Is Falling Apart', The Morning Context (19 July 2023). https://themorningcontext.com/internet/byjus-tuitions-business-is-falling-apart.

188 This was inevitable: Pradip K. Saha, 'Can Mrinal Mohit Be the Fall Guy for Byju's Tuition Centre Chaos?', The Morning Context (8 July 2023). https://themorningcontext.com/internet/can-mrinal-mohit-be-the-fall-guy-for-byjus-tuition-centre-chaos.

189 Now let's take a look at the acquisitions: Pradip K. Saha, 'Davidson Kempner Accuses Byju's of Financial Misconduct, Takes Control of Aakash', The Morning Context (31 July 2023). https://themorningcontext.com/internet/davidson-kempner-accuses-byjus-of-financial-misconduct-takes-control-of-aakash.

189 Great Learning – acquired in 2021 – is currently looking at an annual revenue of ₹800–1,000 crore: Other businesses: Pradip K. Saha, 'Davidson Kempner Accuses Byju's of Financial Misconduct, Takes Control of Aakash', The Morning Context (31 July 2023).

190 Bajaj, the former head of Discovery India, said that he had realized a 'massive gap between the skills needed in the new world and the curriculum in schools': Mathures Paul, 'WhiteHat Jr Shows How to Make Coding Child's Play', *The Telegraph* (8 December

2019). https://www.telegraphindia.com/technology/whitehat-jr-shows-how-to-make-coding-childs-play/cid/1725237?utm_source=dlvr.it&utm_medium=twitter&fbclid=IwAR0FIIjBcje6gU7-EyN8nzZIk3dBJRvEtjQuVEjP9bBCNc_PVmCvqQeEtBE.

191 **It was a dream run:** Ashish K. Mishra, 'A Note on Byju's Acquisition of WhiteHat Jr', The Morning Context (7 August 2020). https://themorningcontext.com/internet/note-byjus-whitehat-jr-acquisition.

192 **In less than six months, it withdrew the suit:** 'WhiteHat Jr Drops Rs 20 Cr Defamation Suit Against Critic Pradeep Poonia', *Business Today* (4 May 2021). https://www.businesstoday.in/latest/corporate/story/whitehat-jr-drops-rs-20-cr-defamation-suit-against-critic-pradeep-poonia-294974-2021-05-04#:~:text=Byju's%2Downed%20WhiteHat%20Jr%20had,misinformation%20about%20the%20start%2Dup&text=Edtech%20start%2Dup%20WhiteHat%20Jr,against%20its%20critic%20Pradeep%20Poonia.

192 **Days before *TechCrunch* reported in February 2023:** Manish Singh, 'Byju's Has Discussed Shutting Down WhiteHat Jr, But Insists on Continuity', *TechCrunch* (23 February 2023). https://techcrunch.com/2023/02/22/byjus-has-discussed-shutting-down-coding-platform-whitehat-jr/.

194 **It is common knowledge that neither the Chaudhrys nor Blackstone was interested in the Byju's deal at first:** Pradip K. Saha, 'Byju's is Pushing Aakash to the Brink', The Morning Context (20 February 2023). https://themorningcontext.com/internet/byjus-is-pushing-aakash-to-the-brink.

194 **Coming together would seemingly have helped both companies:** Pradip K. Saha, 'We felt that with Byju's, we can Redefine Competitive Coaching', The Morning Context (20 April 2021). https://themorningcontext.com/internet/we-felt-that-with-byjus-we-can-redefine-competitive-coaching.

195 **Byju's raised $1.5 billion in a matter of months:** ETtech, 'Byju's Valuation Tops $15 Billion after Over $1-Billion Funding', *The Economic Times* (12 April 2021). https://economictimes.indiatimes.com/tech/startups/byjus-valuation-tops-15-billion-after-over-1-billion-funding/articleshow/82036545.cms?from=mdr.

195 **Byju's, however, didn't make a move to integrate Aakash into its operations:** Pradip K. Saha, 'Byju's Is Pushing Aakash to the Brink', The Morning Context (20 February 2023). https://

themorningcontext.com/internet/byjus-is-pushing-aakash-to-the-brink.

196 **Between 2020 and 2022, Raveendran started four companies in Singapore:** Pradip K. Saha, 'Red Flags in Byju's Still-Incomplete Aakash Acquisition', The Morning Context (19 January 2023). https://themorningcontext.com/internet/red-flags-in-byjus-stillincomplete-aakash-acquisition.

197 **Byju's Pte Ltd is listed as a holding company:** Business profile of Byju's Pte. Ltd, accessed through Singapore's Accounting and Corporate Regulatory Authority in January 2023.

198 **Byju's Investments Pte Ltd was incorporated on 10 May 2022 as a regular private limited company:** Business profile of Byju's Investments Pte. Ltd, accessed through Singapore's Accounting and Corporate Regulatory Authority in January 2023.

198 **Byju's Global Pte Ltd was registered on 6 May 2022 as an exempt private limited company:** Business profile of Byju's Global Pte. Ltd, accessed through Singapore's Accounting and Corporate Regulatory Authority in January 2023.

199 **Finally, let's look at Byju's Holdings 1 Pte Ltd. It was registered on 31 August 2022:** Business profile of Byju's Holdings 1 Pte. Ltd, accessed through Singapore's Accounting and Corporate Regulatory Authority in January 2023.

200 **As things turned out, the final payments for the Aakash deal came from Byju's Investments:** Pradip K. Saha, 'Red Flags in Byju's Still-Incomplete Aakash Acquisition', The Morning Context (19 January 2023). https://themorningcontext.com/internet/red-flags-in-byjus-still-incomplete-aakash-acquisition.

200 **The cheques paid for the Aakash deal had barely cleared:** Pradip K. Saha, 'Byju's Is Pushing Aakash to the Brink', The Morning Context (20 February 2023). https://themorningcontext.com/internet/byjus-is-pushing-aakash-to-the-brink.

201 **Byju's raised ₹2,000 crore (around $250 million) in structured debt:** Deborshi Chaki and Digbijay Mishra, 'Byju's Raises Debt of Rs 2,000 Crore Linked to Future Aakash IPO', The Economic Times (13 May 2023). https://m.economictimes.com/tech/funding/exclusive-byjus-closes-rs-2000-crore-funding-from-davidson-kempner/articleshow/100191031.cms.

201 **we got a tip in July 2023 that the investment fund had accused Byju's of financial misconduct:** Pradip K. Saha, 'Davidson Kempner

Accuses Byju's of Financial Misconduct, Takes Control of Aakash', The Morning Context (31 July 2023). https://themorningcontext. com/internet/davidson-kempner-accuses-byjus-of-financial-misconduct-takes-control-of-aakash.

201 **Byju's accessed ₹400 crore from the ₹2,000 crore loan:** Pradip K. Saha, 'Davidson Kempner Accuses Byju's of Financial Misconduct, Takes Control of Aakash', The Morning Context (31 July 2023).

201 **Sometime between April 2023 and Davidson Kempner taking over the accounts at Aakash:** Pradip K. Saha, 'Byju's Takes Another Rs 300 Crore Out of Aakash', The Morning Context (12 August 2023).

202 **Raveendran incorporated Beeaar Investco Pte. Ltd:** Pradip K. Saha, 'Byju's Takes Another Rs 300 Crore Out of Aakash', The Morning Context (12 August 2023). https://themorningcontext. com/internet/byjus-takes-another-rs-300-crore-out-of-aakash.

205 **Byju's had invoked the unconditional fallback agreement and issued a notice to the Chaudhry family:** PTI, 'Byju's Sends Legal Notice to Aakash Founders Demanding Share Transfer', The Economic Times (1 August 2023). https://economictimes.indiatimes.com/tech/startups/ byjus-sends-legal-notice-to-aakash-founders-demanding-share-transfer/articleshow/102312933.cms?from=mdr.

205 **Blackstone has also dragged its feet:** Pradip K. Saha, 'Aakash Founders to Terminate Share Swap with Byju's', The Morning Context (9 August 2023).

205 **Blackstone and the Chaudhrys issued statements to Byju's:** Pradip K. Saha, 'Aakash Founders to Terminate Share Swap with Byju's', The Morning Context (9 August 2023).

205 **The Chaudhrys have told Byju's that they are terminating their merger and fallback agreement:** Pradip K. Saha, 'Aakash Founders to Terminate Share Swap with Byju's', The Morning Context (9 August 2023). https://themorningcontext.com/internet/aakash-founders-to-terminate-share-swap-with-byjus.

205 **Byju's valuation was slashed by its largest shareholder, Dutchlisted technology investor Prosus:** Pradip K. Saha, 'Prosus Pegs Byju's Valuation at $6 Billion', The Morning Context (23 November 2022). https://themorningcontext.com/internet/prosus-pegs-byjusvaluation-at-6-billion-the-morning-context.

205 **and then to $5.1 billion in June:** Ujjaini Dutta and Diti Pujara, 'Prosus Marks Down Byju's Valuation to $5.1 Bn; Company Claims It Is in Talks to Raise $1 Bn', The Morning Context (28 June 2023). https://

themorningcontext.com/yesterday/prosus-cuts-byjusvaluation-to-
51-bn.

207 **Remember, Raveendran had been talking about a turnover of
₹10,000 crore in FY22:** 'Udayan Mukherjee in Conversation
with Byju Raveendran', *Business Today* (28 August 2021). https://
www.businesstoday.in/news-reel/video/udayan-mukherjee-in-
conversation-with-byju-raveendran-305394-2021-08-28.

207 **The audit process itself didn't begin till June 2023, according to
sources in Byju's, and this led Deloitte Haskins & Sells to resign as
Byju's auditor:** Pranav S. and Pradip K. Saha, 'Byju's Auditor Deloitte
Resigns, No Sign of FY22 Financials', The Morning Context (22
June 2023). https://themorningcontext.com/internet/byjus-auditor-
deloitte-resigns-no-sign-of-fy22-financials.

208 **The financial statements of the Company for the year ended March
31, 2022 are long delayed:** Deloitte Haskins & Sells's resignation
letter to Byju's board of directors, dated 22 June 2023, accessed
through the ministry of corporate affairs website.

208 **all quit the Byju's board without citing any reasons:** Samidha
Sharma and Digbijay Mishra, 'More Trouble for Byju's as Three
Board Members, Auditor Deloitte Resign', *The Economic Times* (22
June 2023). https://economictimes.indiatimes.com/tech/startups/
more-trouble-for-byjus-as-key-board-members-resign-sources/
articleshow/101191922.cms.

209 **Byju's response?:** Samidha Sharma and Digbijay Mishra, 'More
Trouble for Byju's as Three Board Members, Auditor Deloitte
Resign', *The Economic Times* (22 June 2023). https://economictimes.
indiatimes.com/tech/startups/more-trouble-for-byjus-as-key-
board-members-resign-sources/articleshow/101191922.cms.

209 **then claimed that the exits had been planned beforehand:** ETTech,
'Peak XV, Prosus and Chan Zuckerberg Confirm Exit from Byju's
Board', *The Economic Times* (24 July 2023). https://economictimes.
indiatimes.com/tech/startups/prosus-peak-xv-confirm-resignation-
of-representatives-from-byjus-board/articleshow/101224957.
cms?from=mdr.

209 **Prosus and Peak XV have confirmed that their representatives quit
the edtech company's board:**
— 'Exited Byju's Board, Say Peak XV, Prosus, CZI', *Mint* (23 June
2023). https://www.livemint.com/companies/news/exited-byju-s-
board-say-peak-xv-prosus-11687541899651.html.

— Ujjaini Dutta and Diti Pujara, 'Byju's Leadership Comes in For Stick for the Way It Operates', The Morning Context (26 July 2023).

209 **Prosus said that Byju's leadership regularly 'disregarded advice:** Ujjaini Dutta and Diti Pujara, 'Byju's Leadership "Disregarded Advice" from Board Members', The Morning Context (26 July 2023). https://themorningcontext.com/yesterday/byjus-leadership-comes-in-for-stick-for-the-way-it-operates.

209 **Peak XV Partners, the edtech firm's second-largest investor, told its limited partners:** Ujjaini Dutta and Diti Pujara, 'Byju's Leadership Comes in for Stick for the Way It Operates,' The Morning Context (26 July 2023).

Chapter 11

212 **The *Economic Times* reported in September that Byju's is in talks:** Digbijay Mishra, 'Byju's Puts Epic, Great Learning on Sale to Clear $1.2 Billion Loan', *The Economic Times* (12 September 2023).

212 **it still might not be enough to put the company back on a sustainable footing:** Pradip K. Saha, 'Selling Epic and Great Learning Won't Solve Byju's Cash Flow Problem', The Morning Context (20 September 2023).

212 **In October 2023, lenders of the $1.2 billion term loan appointed risk advisory firm Kroll:** Sneha Shah, 'Byju's lenders appoint Kroll to Help Safeguard Assets of Great Learning, Singapore entity', *Mint* (11 October 2023). https://www.livemint.com/companies/news/kroll-appointed-to-help-safeguard-byjus-and-great-learning-education-details-here-11697006138995.html.

212 **Kroll, in turn, placed Great Learning into receivership in Singapore:** Reshmi Basu, Anto Antony, and Megawati Wijaya, 'Byju's Lenders Move to Put Singapore Unit in Receivership', Bloomberg (11 October 2023). https://www.bloomberg.com/news/articles/2023-10-11/byju-s-lenders-move-to-put-unit-in-receivership-after-default.

214 **three-paragraph press statement:** Sankalp Phartiyal, Anto Antony, Bloomberg: 'Byju's Reveals ₹2,250 Crore Loss Amid Deepening Debt Dispute', NDTV.com (5 November 2023). https://www.ndtv.com/india-news/byjus-reveals-rs-2-250-crore-loss-amid-deepening-debt-dispute-4546636.

215 **Raveendran's claims of generating $1 billion in India revenue in 2020–21:** Manish Singh, 'Indian Decacorn Byju's CEO Talks

About Future Acquisitions, Coronavirus and International Expansion', *TechCrunch* (15 September 2020). https://techcrunch.com/2020/09/15/indian-decacorn-byjus-ceo-talks-about-future-acquisitions-coronavirus-and-international-expansion/.

215 **and ₹10,000 crore in FY22:** 'Byju's Posts Gross Revenue of Rs 10,000 crore in FY22', *Livemint* (14 September 2022). https://www.livemint.com/companies/company-results/byjus-posts-gross-revenue-of-rs-10-000-crore-in-fy22-11663151145450.html.

219 **Its promoters – founder Byju Raveendran, his brother Riju Ravindran and Byju's wife, Divya Gokulnath – have together sold shares worth around $408.53 million:** Ujjaini Dutta and Diti Pujara, 'Byju's Promoters Sold Shares Worth $408.53 Mn Since 2015: PrivateCircle Research', The Morning Context (4 July 2023). https://themorningcontext.com/yesterday/the-byjus-sold-shares-worth-over-400-mn-over-8-years.

225 **With more than 150 million registered users, Byju's, for example, only had 7 million paid subscribers:** Byju's Press Release, 'BYJU'S is On a Path to Profitability; Targets to Achieve it by March 2023' (12 October 2022). https://byjus.com/press/byjus-is-on-a-path-to-profitability-targets-to-achieve-it-by-march-2023/#:~:text=About%20BYJU'S&text=With%20over%20150%20million%20registered,for%20students%20around%20the%20world.

Acknowledgements

People say writing a book is like a journey. I didn't understand this before embarking upon one. I won't be here without the following people.

This book wouldn't have been possible without Ashish K. Mishra and The Morning Context. Our careers started around the same time but followed different trajectories. By the time we collaborated, Ashish was a hotshot writer and editor, and I was, after a long stint in copyediting, finding my feet in long-form feature writing. God knows what gave Ashish the courage to ask me to cover start-ups, that too edtech, which was the sunshine sector back in 2020. Without him, I wouldn't be writing on the subject.

Thank you Chiki Sarkar, for trusting a debutant with this book. Devangshu Datta, my editor at Juggernaut, not just for his careful edits to give the book shape but for not losing his patience with me, despite the delays. To Devangana Ojha and Oorja Mishra, for their keen eye for detail and careful copyediting.

I wish I had known Prem Panicker earlier in my journey as a journalist. But better late than never. Over the past few years, we have talked about writing, of course, but also many things outside work, from the mundane to the existential, and he has always had a quick answer to all my queries, including whether I should take up this book.

When I told Ranjeet Singh, my Hindi teacher from high school, about the book in November 2022, he said: 'This is the first milestone in the journey you had started more than two decades ago.' He knows because he was there at the start and has been my North Star since.

I am grateful to some good editors I had the fortune to work with. Sidin Vadukut gave me the first opportunity to write. 'Write,' he would say. 'Just because everyone tells the story doesn't mean you don't have to. Do it and give it your best shot.' We often argued, but his contribution to my career will always be invaluable.

Sukumar Ranganathan, the current editor of *Hindustan Times*, for always being benevolent and accommodating. In his previous role as the editor of *Mint*, he kept moving me to different desks and teams, giving me the opportunity to learn on the go. When I got bored of copyediting and found another gig that would give me the opportunity to write, he stopped me from leaving. 'Do whatever you want to do and do it here,' he had said. I chose *Mint Lounge*. He agreed. How that happened, I may never know.

Rajesh Jose who, after the initial bullying, became my friend and guide at *Mint*, and beyond. I am grateful to friends and wonderful colleagues – former and present – who not only indulged me with their stories, thoughts and good food, but also helped me with context, contacts and counsel, time and again.

Friends. Shreyas Sharma who became my first friend

in Delhi in the summer of 2006, while reciting Harivansh Rai Bachchan's 'Madhushala' in the corridors of Delhi University's Art Faculty, and has since then remained a constant in my life. Our shared love for Galib-Gulzar-Bachchan, Kishore-Pancham-Gulzar, the Ganga and Bhojpuri, cemented that friendship. Neil Rodricks, the colleague who became a friend, my gateway to rock music, world cinema, psychological thrillers and Goan food. We will do the road trip to Goa soon.

To the people I have deeply loved and lost, to death, and to life. Vishnu Gupta, who started as my landlord but whose home became my home, my permanent address in Delhi – my first permanent address ever. Vishnu bhaiya, you left us in 2022, but your innocent optimism and faith in me keep me going.

Writing on education/edtech and then writing this book have made me think a lot about Indian parents. I see their constraints and insecurities, their collective struggle to shape a better future for their children and their unyielding courage in the relentless pursuit of that goal, in a new light. It makes me feel fortunate to have the parents I do. Ma and Baba, thank you, for without you, there would be no me. You gave Pallavi and me what you didn't have – a secure childhood and the courage to go out and do what we wanted. I wish you were here, Baba. My mother-in-law, Rita Rao, one of the strongest women I have ever known, whose perseverance and grit reflects in her two daughters – Jyotsna and Namrata.

Namrata, my wife, the love of my life. I was a small-town boy, ignorant and, often, arrogant, out of my depth in the world outside. You became my rock, my anchor. You are the first editor of all my first drafts, my biggest fan, my fiercest critic, my best friend; I could write this book only because you took charge of everything else, invisibly. I can say a million thank yous and they still won't be enough. From being tag-team partners, scouting for letters to the editor at *Deccan Chronicle* in 2007, to arguing about the haircut for our son, we have come a long way. It's been quite a ride and I wouldn't have it any other way.

Finally, my darling son Abhigyaan. You are the light of my eyes, the colours of my rainbow, my sunshine and joy. Your shining smile, adorable laughs and endless energy have turned each of the 1,595 days we have spent together so far, magical. If you ever need a little reminder of how wonderful you are, I hope you open this book and see.

A special thank you to all my sources, entrepreneurs, industry experts and the hundreds of employees – former and current – at Byju's who cared enough about the integrity of our work and the future of children to entrust me with their perspective, and valuable information, sometimes even at the cost of losing their jobs. Many of them spent hours, days and months, explaining concepts, taking questions and helping me understand the workings of edtech. Here, I must mention Pratik Makhija and Devaraju N.R., the two people who went on the record for this book.

I can't sign off without thanking my readers whose sincerity and feedback have not only kept me on the ball, and grounded, but also motivated me when the going got tough. I am because of you.

A Note on the Author

Author portrait: Priyanka Parashar

Pradip K. Saha is a journalist and writer. He is a co-founder of The Morning Context, where he writes primarily on education technology, but also on mobility and the gig economy. His prior associations include the *Deccan Chronicle* and *Mint*. This is his first book.